STRATEGY IMPLEMENTATION

THE WEST SERIES IN STRATEGIC MANAGEMENT

Consulting Editor
Charles W. Hofer

Second Edition

STRATEGY IMPLEMENTATION
STRUCTURE, SYSTEMS, AND PROCESS

Jay R. Galbraith
MANAGEMENT CONSULTANTS, LTD.

Robert K. Kazanjian
THE UNIVERSITY OF MICHIGAN

WEST PUBLISHING COMPANY
St. Paul   New York   Los Angeles   San Francisco

Copyediting by Joan Torkildson

Interior art by Alice B. Thiede, Carto-Graphics

Cover design by Peter Thiel, Kim Rafferty

Typesetting by Huron Valley Graphics, Inc. Typefaces are Aster and Optima.

Index by Lois Oster

Library of Congress Cataloging-in-Publication Data

Galbraith, Jay R.
  Strategy implementation.

  (West series in strategic management)
  Bibliography: p.
  Includes index.
  1. Organization.   2. Organizational effectiveness.
3. Corporate planning.   I. Kazanjian, Robert K.
II. Title.   III. Series.
HD31.G248   1986   658.4'012   86-24
ISBN 0-314-85236-0

1st Reprint—1987

To our parents, whose encouragement, guidance, and support have enabled us to grow and to fulfill our potential.

CONTENTS

4

Implementing Diversification Strategies: An Alternative Framework   *46*

5

Processes and Systems for Managing Diversity   *71*

6

Strategy, People, and Rewards   *91*

7

Integration of Dimensions for Strategy Implementation   *108*

8

Strategic Adaptation Models   *124*

9

Strategy and Organization: State of the Art   *145*

References   *171*

Index   *181*

FOREWORD

This series is a response to the rapid and significant changes that have occurred in the strategic management/business policy area over the past twenty-five years. Although strategic management/ business policy is a subject of long standing in management schools, it was traditionally viewed as a capstone course whose primary purpose was to *integrate* the knowledge and skills students had gained in the functional disciplines. During the past fifteen years, however, strategic management/business policy has developed a substantive content of its own. Originally, this content focused on the concepts of corporate and business strategies and on the processes by which such strategies were formulated and implemented within organizations. More recently, as Figure 1 and Table 1 illustrate, the scope of the field has broadened to include the study of both the functions and responsibilities of top management and the organizational systems and processes used to establish overall organizational goals and objectives and to formulate, implement, and control the strategies and policies necessary to achieve these goals and objectives.

When the *West Series in Business Policy and Planning* was originally published, most of the texts in the field did not yet reflect this extension in scope. The principal purpose of the original series was, therefore, to fill this void by incorporating the latest research findings and conceptual thought in the field into each of the texts in the series. In the intervening seven years, the series has succeeded to a far greater degree than we could have ever hoped.

However, the pace of research in strategic management/business policy has, if anything, increased since the publication of the original series. Some changes are, thus, clearly in order. It is the purpose of the *West Series in Strategic Management* to continue the tradition

Figure 1   The Evolution of Business Policy/Strategic Management As a Field of Study

The Traditional Boundary of Business Policy

The Current Boundaries of Strategic Management

Some Major Contributors to the Redefinition of the Field

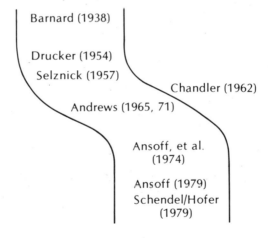

Barnard (1938)

Drucker (1954)
Selznick (1957)

Chandler (1962)

Andrews (1965, 71)

Ansoff, et al. (1974)

Ansoff (1979)
Schendel/Hofer (1979)

of innovative, state-of-the-art coverage of the field of strategic management started by the *West Series in Business Policy and Planning* both through revisions to all the books in the original series and through the addition of two new titles. In making such revisions, care has been taken to ensure not only that the various texts fit together as a series, but also that each is self-contained and addresses a major topic in the field. In addition, the series has been designed so that it covers almost all the major topics that form the

Table 1   The Major Subfields of Business Policy/Strategic Management

    1. Boards of Directors

    2. The Nature of General Management Work

    3. Middle-Level General Management

    4. Stakeholder Analysis

    5. Organizational Goal Formulation

    6. Corporate Social Policy and Management Ethics

    7. Macroenvironmental Analysis

*   8. Strategy Formulation and Strategic Decision Making

*   9. Corporate-Level Strategy (including Mergers, Acquisitions, and Divestitures)

   10. Business-Level Strategy

   11. Strategic Planning and Information Systems

 ⤺ 12. The Strategy-Structure-Performance Linkage

 ⤺ 13. The Design of Macroorganizational Structure and Systems

   14. Strategic Control Systems

* 15. Organizational Culture

* 16. Leadership Style for General Managers

   17. The Strategic Management of Small Businesses and New Ventures

   18. The Strategic Management of High Tech Organizations

   19. The Strategic Management of Not-for-Profit Organizations

⤺ Indicates subfields that are covered extensively by this text

*   Indicates other subfields that are discussed in this text

heartland of strategic management, as Figure 2 illustrates. The individual texts in the series are

Setting Strategic Goals and Objectives, 2d ed.
Max D. Richards

Strategy Formulation: Issues and Concepts
Charles W. Hofer

Strategy Formulation: Power and Politics, 2d ed.
Ian C. MacMillan and Patricia E. Jones

Strategy Implementation: Structure, Systems, and Process, 2d ed.
Jay R. Galbraith and Robert K. Kazanjian

Strategic Control
Peter Lorange, Michael F. Scott Morton, and Sumantra Ghoshal

Macroenvironmental Analysis for Strategic Management
Liam Fahey and V. K. Narayanan

Figure 2 **The Strategic Management Process**

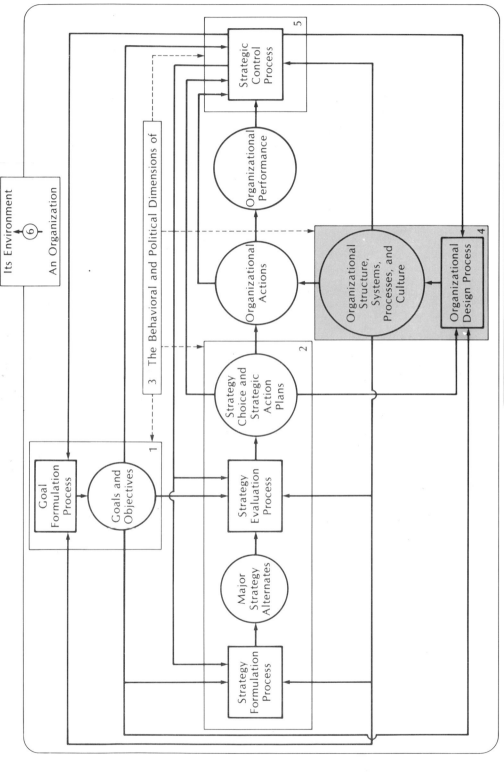

1. Setting Strategic Goals and Objectives, 2d ed.
2. Strategy Formulation: Issues and Concepts
3. Strategy Formulation: Power and Politics, 2d ed.

4. Strategy Implementation: Structure, Systems, and Process, 2d ed.
5. Strategic Control
6. Macroenvironmental Analysis for Strategic Management

The series has also been designed so that the texts within it can be used in several ways. First, the entire series can be used as a set to provide an advanced conceptual overview of the field of strategic management. Second, selected texts in the series can be combined with cases drawn from the Harvard Case Services, the Case Teaching Association, and/or the Case Research Association to create a course customized to particular instructor needs. Third, individual texts in the series can be used to supplement the conceptual materials contained in the existing text and casebooks in the field. The series thus offers the individual instructor great flexibility in designing the required business policy/strategic management course. Fourth, because of their self-contained nature, each of the texts can be used either individually or in combination with other materials as the basis for an advanced specialized course in strategic management. For instance, the text on *Strategic Control* could be used to create a state-of-the-art course on "Strategic Control Systems." Likewise, the *Macroenvironmental Analysis for Strategic Management* and *Strategy Formulation: Power and Politics* texts could be combined to create an innovative course on "Stakeholder Management." Or the text on *Setting Strategic Goals and Objectives* could be combined with a text on boards of directors to create an advanced course on the latter topic.

Finally, in concluding this Common Foreword I would like to thank my co-editor on the original series, Dan Schendel of Purdue University, for his efforts on that series. They were both substantial and valuable. Indeed, the series could not have been established as effectively as it was without him.

Charles W. Hofer
Editor
October 1985

PREFACE

This book deals with issues of organization design directed toward strategy implementation. It is intended as a text for advanced undergraduate and MBA policy courses, but clearly has relevance for the practicing organization designer as well. Much of our work is based upon the conceptual frameworks and empirical studies triggered by Alfred Chandler's *Strategy and Structure* (1962). Initially, such works proposed that the structure of the organization should reflect the product-market strategy of the firm. We depart from Chandler and other early works by expanding the notion of organization to include more than just departmental structure and the degree of centralization. Working from a broader definition, we demonstrate how strategy must be matched with a compatible, congruent configuration of organizational structure, process, systems, and people for effective financial performance to result. Subsequent to Chandler, a considerable body of literature has emerged in the fields of strategic management, economics, and organization theory to test and extend his thesis. Where supported by a solid research base, we offer prescriptive statements regarding the relationship of strategy to various organizational elements. In some areas, however, research has not yet progressed to the level that makes such statements advisable.

Consistent with the preceding, we also argue that the move from one strategy to another requires a disengaging, realignment, and reconnecting of all organizational factors. In this book we discuss various organizational forms that can result from such efforts. Although we discuss issues of strategic adaptation, the problem of managing the transition from one form to another is not central to this work. Instead, we concentrate upon conditions under which one form would be preferable to another.

In addition to reviewing the state of the art of our knowledge about strategy and organization as embodied in various literatures, this volume of the *West Series in Strategic Management* also looks at the organizational and administrative innovations currently unfolding in the field. Just as Chandler profiled General Motors and Du Pont in their invention of the multidivisional form in the 1920s, we have searched for new forms that appear to be responsive to the competitive challenges of the 1980s and beyond. In this regard, we discuss the organizational configurations not suited to the management of diversity. This includes a review of matrix organizations, currently out of favor but nonetheless suited to the problem. Second, we discuss various evolving, complex organizational forms employed in the globalization strategies of numerous diversified firms. Here, we discuss the emergence of network organizations that include such designs as joint ventures and cooperative production, distribution, and research agreements which are, for example, increasingly observable in industries where competition is global. Finally, we present organizational arrangements being used by firms to encourage, nurture, and reinforce innovation and entrepreneurship. For the most part, the firms developing and institutionalizing these administrative innovations are pursuing highly diverse strategies, as they are typically large multiproduct, multimarket, multinational enterprises.

We acknowledge the support and advice of a number of individuals who played a role in the preparation of this work. First, Chuck Hofer helped considerably with his extensive review of the previous edition and his numerous suggestions for refinement and extension. Daniel A. Nathanson of Vernitron Corporation provided a thorough review of Chapters 2 and 3, with strong suggestions for additions and clarification. Additionally, thanks go to the reviewers of the manuscript: Anil K. Gupta of Boston University, Gary B. Roberts of Kennesaw College, and William A. Jones, Jr., of Georgia State University. Each of these people contributed to the enhancement of the final version. Any errors of commission or omission rest with the authors. Praveen Nayyar and Karen Bantel, both doctoral students at the University of Michigan, were extremely helpful in conducting literature reviews, proofreading, and related tasks. Donna Scott, Betty Wolverton, and Joan Walker deserve special thanks for their word processing of the manuscript in accordance with our usual unrealistic deadlines. Finally, we want to thank our families for their understanding and continuous support during the ups and downs of completing the book.

STRATEGY IMPLEMENTATION

1

Introduction

This chapter presents an overview of the book by introducing an overall framework along with some important concepts and key definitions. The basic premise with which we begin is that an organization has a variety of structural forms and organizational processes from which to choose when implementing a particular strategy. Our contention is that the choice of structural forms makes an economic difference; that is, all structural forms are not equally effective in implementing a given strategy. Therefore, organization members should allocate the time and effort necessary to plan their organizational form, just as time and effort are allocated for the formulation of strategic and other plans.

However, in addition to structure, other design variables should be considered if a firm is to marshal its resources effectively and implement its strategy. The organization must be designed to facilitate the proper selection, training, and development of its people. Individuals must be able to perform their tasks and thereby carry out the desired strategy. Congruent reward systems must provide the incentives necessary for people to work effectively and in harmony with the organization's goals. Information must also be available to control and coordinate activities, to measure performance effectively, and to monitor and plan. Hence, the choice of organizational form consists of a comprehensive design of structure, systems, and processes. The major design variables that are presented in this book are represented schematically in Figure 1.1.

Each of the variables depicted in Figure 1.1 represents a choice for the organization. However, to be successful, the choices should be internally consistent and also consistent with the firm's product-market strategy. The general finding has been that structural choice follows from strategic choice. The decision to make a change in

1

Figure 1.1 Schematic Showing Fit among Major Organization Design Variables

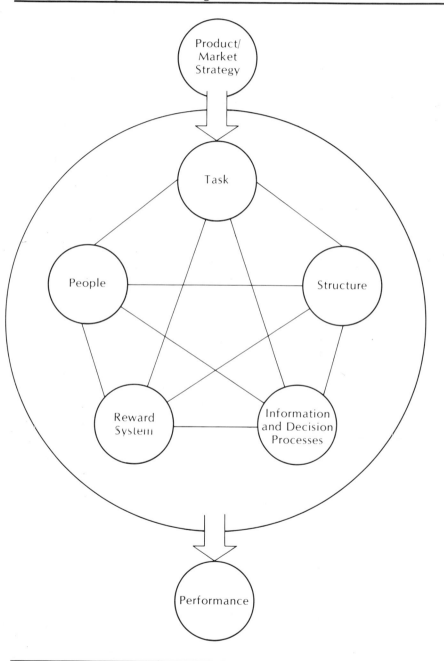

strategy often calls for a change in the entire set of design variables. The process is one of constant readjustment.

We have mentioned the terms *strategy*, *structure*, and *process*. Examining these terms more precisely is essential before we delve into the relationships between them.

DEFINITIONS

The word *strategy*, which derives from the ancient Greek word *strategos*, meaning "the art of the general," has since taken on a variety of broad and often ambiguous definitions. For instance, in game theory, strategy is concerned principally with a statistical set of rules for the player to improve the probabilities of a desired payoff. In this book, however, we are concerned with strategy as specific directions and actions emanating from the strategy formulation process.

We concur, then, with Hofer and Schendel (1978), who define an organization's strategy as the fundamental pattern of present and planned resource deployments and environmental interactions that indicate how the organization will achieve its objectives. Embedded within this definition are two prime components of strategy. *Scope*, sometimes called domain, refers to the breadth of activity pursued by the firm and is typically captured in terms of product-market diversity. *Resource deployment*, which sets levels and patterns of resources and skills, ultimately defines the organization's distinctive competence. (For a more detailed statement of the concept of strategy and associated analytic constructs, see Hofer and Schendel [1978], which is a companion volume in this series.)

It becomes apparent, then, that different strategies can be identified at various points in time for large-scale organizations. In his book *Strategy and Structure* (1962) Alfred D. Chandler distinguished certain key growth strategies that were most important for ensuring the long-term survival of the organization. These strategies, identified in Table 1.1, are expansion of volume, geographic dispersion, vertical integration, and product diversification. Chandler showed how each strategy posed a different type of administrative difficulty and therefore tended to lead to a different form of organizational structure. Many theorists in various disciplines have dealt with these same strategies and with the same basic issue of the strategy-structure fit shown in Figure 1.2.

This book reviews the work of Chandler and of theorists in areas such as economics, sociology, business policy, and organizational behavior. Although the vocabulary of each field differs somewhat, many similarities between them can be pinpointed.

Table 1.1   Chandler's Key Growth Strategies

EXPANSION OF VOLUME
   Increased sales within existing market

GEOGRAPHIC DISPERSION
   Entry in geographically distinct markets with existing
   product or service

VERTICAL INTEGRATION
   Movement up and/or down the value-added chain through
   the absorption of supplier or buyer tasks

PRODUCT DIVERSIFICATION
   Development of new products or businesses, typically
   described in terms of degree of relatedness to existing
   activities of the firm

The first growth strategy that Chandler discussed—expansion of volume—refers to increased sales in a single market or in existing markets, whereas geographic diversification (the second strategy) is the entry into geographically different markets. Vertical integration represents the third growth strategy and is characterized by the firm's absorption of its suppliers or industrial customers. Therefore, the major activities of these vertically integrated companies usually consist of stages in the sequential processing of a particular material from its raw form to a finished product (Scott 1971; Rumelt 1974). A simplified diagram of a vertically integrated oil company is shown in Figure 1.3.

The strategies of product and market diversification represent the major direction of research and attention in this book. As will be shown, product diversified firms have become the dominant type of organization, not only in the United States but also abroad. Chandler

Figure 1.2   The Strategy-Structure Fit

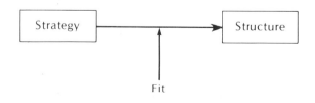

Figure 1.3   Simplified Diagram of a Vertically Integrated Oil Company

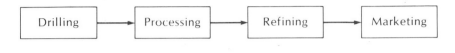

defines diversification as the development of new products. Other theorists, such as Leonard Wrigley (1970) and Richard Rumelt (1974), subsequently refined the concept by classifying four types of diversification. The first is single-product business, which includes firms such as Maytag, makers of washing machines and dryers, and Wrigley, the chewing gum manufacturers. The next category is the dominant business, in which one product accounts for 70 to 95 percent of the firm's total sales. Examples include most of the oil companies: Mobil, Atlantic Richfield, and Exxon, to name a few. Their dominant product is oil, but they have diversified vertically and into related businesses such as plastics, petrochemicals, fertilizers, coal, and atomic energy. Other examples include Philip Morris, which has added beer, gum, razor blades, toiletries, hospital and surgical supplies, and other products to its dominant business of cigarettes and tobacco, and Campbell Soup, which has added baked goods and candy to its dominant canned soup business. The related product business represents the third category. Firms in this category have diversified more than 30 percent of their sales outside their main business, but they have done so by selling products related by common customer, distribution channels, technology, or some other factor. That is, some connection existed between the products. An example is Dow-Corning, which diversified its product line but remained with products that used silicon chemistry. Other examples include Du Pont, General Electric, General Foods, General Mills, Gillette, Johnson and Johnson, Procter and Gamble, and Westinghouse. The final category is the unrelated business organization. Here, the firms have more than 30 percent of their sales outside their main business, but these other businesses have little or no relation to each other. Examples of such firms include Colt Industries, Curtiss-Wright, FMC, Litton Industries, and Rockwell Manufacturing. These different types of diversification strategies have been shown to have different effects on organizational structure and process.

What, then, is meant by the terms *structure* and *process*? Chandler defines structure (1962, 14) as the design of organization through which the enterprise is administered. He goes on to state, "the design, whether formally or informally defined has two aspects: first the lines of authority and communication between the different administrative offices and officers and second the information and data that flow through these lines of communication and authority." Organization theorists such as John Child (1972) define structures as the formal allocation of work roles and the administrative mechanisms to control and integrate work activity, including those that cross formal organizational boundaries. We view structures as the segmentation of work into roles such as production, finance, marketing, and so on; the recombining of roles into departments or divisions around functions, products, regions, or markets; and the distribution of power across this role structure. We view processes as the direction and frequency of work and information flows linking the differentiated roles within and between departments of complex organization.

Several structural types exist, including the centralized functional organization, the decentralized multidivisional form, the holding company form, and the more recently developed matrix form. A centralized organization is characterized by the locus of power concentrated at the top of the organization. Conversely, a decentralized organization is one in which power and decision-making authority are more evenly dispersed throughout the hierarchy and can be found at lower levels in the organization. The functional organization is usually more centralized, and its departments are specialized and arranged by function, such as marketing, finance, manufacturing, and legal. Organization charts representing the functional, multidivisional, holding company, and matrix structures are shown in Figures 1.4 through 1.7 respectively. (Three of these figures are drawn from actual firms and are not intended to depict the current organizational forms of these enterprises, but are intended more to serve as representatives examples of these generic structures.)

The multidivisional organization is generally more decentralized than the functional organization, because the departments are separated on the basis of product, market, or region. Usually, all the resources necessary to manufacture and sell the product or to supply the market are put under the control of a particular division. The division manager is therefore given considerable authority and responsibility. The holding company form is one in which even greater authority and responsibility are given to the divisions. The corporate office is smaller than that of the multidivisional firm because the corporate office merely performs the function of capital allocation. Finally, the matrix organization, represented in Figure 1.7, reflects both a function and a product orientation. Many variations to the structure just mentioned exist and will be discussed. This presentation was made merely to introduce the concepts in an understandable fashion.

Figure 1.4   A Functional Organization (The Dictaphone Corporation)

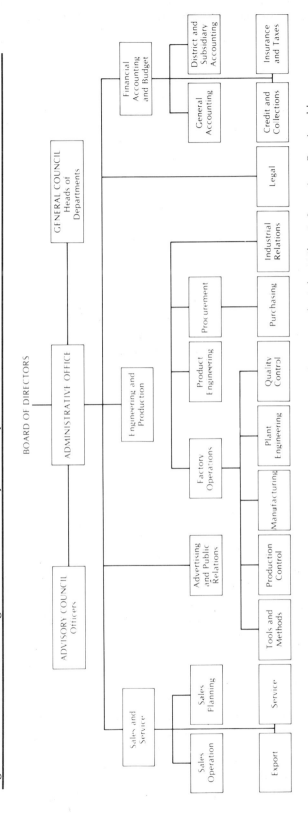

Source: From Joseph A. Litterer, *Organizations: Structure and Behavior.* Copyright © 1963 by John Wiley & Sons, Inc. Reprinted by permission of John Wiley & Sons, Inc.

Figure 1.5   A Multidivisional Structure at Texas Instruments

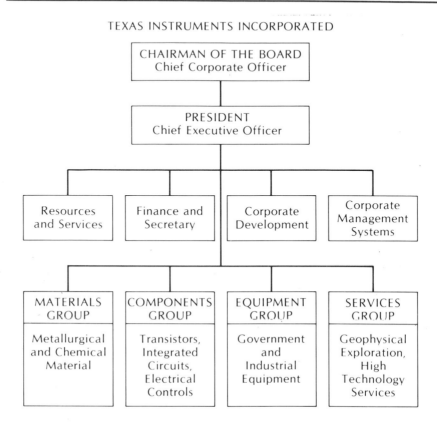

TEXAS INSTRUMENTS INCORPORATED

Source: This figure appears in the case Innovation at Texas Instruments, 9-672-036. Copyright © 1971 by the President and Fellows of Harvard College. Reproduced by permission.

Now that we have defined the terms *strategy, structure,* and *process,* albeit briefly, we are able to introduce some of the major concepts, issues, hypotheses, and theories that are presented in this book.

CONCEPTS, ISSUES, HYPOTHESES, AND THEORIES

Chandler's general thesis is that structure follows strategy. Changes in a firm's strategy result from an awareness of the opportunities and needs—created by changing population, income, and technology—to

Figure 1.6   Hypothetical Unrelated Business Corporation

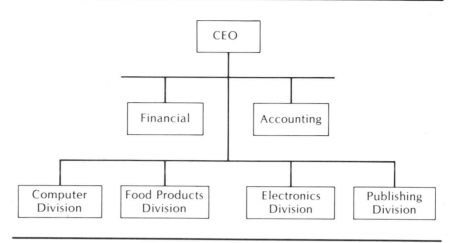

employ existing or expanding resources more profitably. The new strategy brings about new administrative problems, however. These new administrative problems require a new, or at least a refashioned, structure if the enlarged enterprise is to operate efficiently.

Our prior examples illustrate some of the main strategy-structure relationships. Basically, the firms with single- and dominant-product strategies utilize the functional form illustrated by the Dictaphone Corporation (currently part of Pitney-Bowes) in Figure 1 4 Similarly, most related business firms such as Texas Instruments have a multi-divisional structure. Finally, most unrelated product firms generally use the holding company form. Therefore, as we move from the single-product firm to the unrelated firm, we also see a move from centralization to decentralization. The greater decentralization is presumably needed to cope with the additional uncertainty and diversity presented by the firm's product-market strategy.

Chandler's thesis, then, represents what is currently known in the organization field as a contingency theory. Contingency theory states that there is no one best way to organize, but that all ways of organizing are not equally effective (Galbraith 1973). The choice is dependent or contingent upon something. Chandler suggests that structure is contingent upon the growth strategy. Subsequent theorists have elaborated upon this idea and added some other contingencies. Thus, the greater the diversity among products or markets or both, the greater the likelihood that the successful organization will be multidivisional as opposed to functional. Moreover, with greater diversity, decision-making power for operations is more

Figure 1.7   The Dow-Corning Matrix

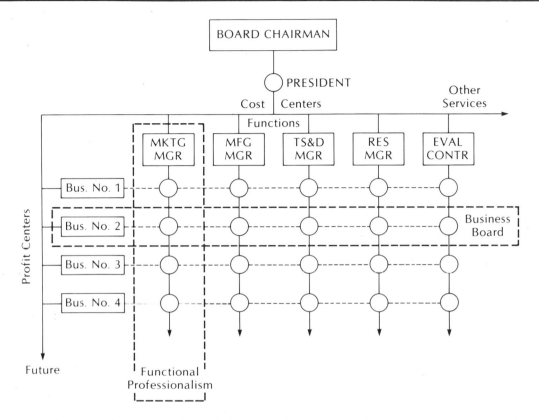

likely to be concentrated at lower levels in the successful organization. The research and analysis supporting these statements are presented in the next three chapters.

The design of the organization is more than a choice of alternative divisional structures. This point is illustrated in Figure 1.1, where structure is but one dimension of the organizational form that intervenes between strategy and performance. However, other dimensions such as resource allocation processes, information systems, cross-departmental decision processes, career paths, and reward systems have not received the same level of research attention that has been accorded to structure, although the body of work in these areas is growing. Only recently has there been any attempt to match variations in these systems and processes with variations in strategy. But little work to date has investigated the relationship of these variables and strategy to performance. Therefore, the smaller amount of attention given them reflects only the research that has been conducted, not the intrinsic importance of these dimensions. In any case, our belief is that variation in strategy should be matched with variation in processes and systems as well as in structure in order for organizations to implement strategies successfully. The specific ways in which these dimensions should vary are described in Chapters 5 and 6.

The key concept and hypothesis that we present is that of consistency or fit and its relation to effectiveness. That is, the design problem is more than one of matching strategy and structure and matching processes and strategy. It requires matching all these dimensions to one another as well as to strategy in order to achieve a fit, a consistency, or a congruence among all organizational dimensions. We regard the achievement of fit as the most important feature of the contribution of organization to economic effectiveness. This concept is dealt with in more detail in Chapter 7.

As a consequence of the relation between consistency and performance, the design and redesign of organizations is a massive undertaking requiring substantial time and effort. Therefore, each major change has been hypothesized as constituting a different stage of organizational development. Several authors as well as Chandler have proposed such stagewise growth models to explain the development of corporate structures of U.S. firms. Alternatively, other views of how firms adapt over time to changing environmental and industry conditions have been offered as well. These models are reviewed and analyzed in Chapter 8. Questions naturally emerge from the discussion of strategic adaptation. Are there stages beyond those described by Chandler and others? Are emerging organizational forms such as network organizations or various matrix configurations employed by firms pursuing global strategies reflective of a more advanced state of corporate management practice? How do large, complex organizations maintain an innovative, entrepreneurial capability? The current state of the art in organizational structure, process, and related variables regarding these and other issues is analyzed in Chapter 9. These advances are described and discussed with respect to consistency between strategy and organization.

SUMMARY AND MANAGERIAL IMPLICATIONS

This chapter introduced the major concepts to be used in this book in order to provide common definitions for discussing strategy, structure, and other components of organization. Strategy was defined, and four specific types of strategy were identified. Four alternative structures were also enumerated, together with various organizational processes. The main emphasis was that the firm must achieve a fit between its strategy and its primary organizational elements. The achievement of this fit, or the lack thereof, is hypothesized as having an economic impact that is crucial, especially under competitive conditions. The theoretical foundations and research support for the strategy-structure portion of this hypothesis are presented in the next two chapters. Managerial implications and recommendations are offered as well.

2

Conceptual and Empirical Foundations of Strategy and Structure

In this chapter, the conceptual foundations of the strategy and structure linkage are presented by reviewing the works of Chandler and Williamson. Chandler's historical study *Strategy and Structure* has stimulated conceptual and empirical works of an interdisciplinary nature. Williamson, an economist, discusses the divisionalized firm and its ability to internalize the market mechanism. Subsequent empirical research investigating and defining the influence of strategy on structure is also presented.

CHANDLER'S THESIS: STRATEGY AND STRUCTURE

The recent and increasing scholarly interest in strategy and structure connections outside of business policy textbooks was impelled by the publication of Chandler's research in *Strategy and Structure* (Chandler 1962). On the basis of a historical study of seventy of America's largest firms, he formulated several hypotheses that stimulated much of the subsequent work. First, he proposed the principle that organizational structure follows the growth strategy of the firm. Second, he proposed a stagewise developmental sequence for the strategies and structures of American enterprises. Third, he theorized that organizations do not change their structures until they are provoked by inefficiency to do so. In part, this is because the formulator of strategies is rarely the creator of organizations. Let us look briefly at each of these points prior to reviewing the studies that followed from them.

Chandler's work is best known for the hypothesis that is suggested in the title of his book. "The thesis deduced from these several propositions is then that structure follows strategy and that the most complex type of structure is the result of the concatenation of several basic strategies." (Chandler 1962, 14) Thus, the structure of an organization follows from its growth strategy. Specifically, as organizations change their growth strategy to employ resources more profitably in the face of changing technology, income, and population, the new strategy poses new administrative problems. These administrative problems are solved only by refashioning the organizational structure to fit the new strategy. A corollary to this thesis is that if a structural adjustment does not take place, the strategy will not be completely effective, and economic inefficiency will result. Chandler proposed a sequence consisting of new strategy creation, emergence of new administrative problems, decline in economic performance, invention of a new appropriate structure, and subsequent recovery to profitable levels.

In his historical study, the prior sequence was seen to be repeated often as American firms grew and changed their growth strategies. Initially, most firms were units such as plants, sales offices, or warehouses in a single industry, a single location, and a single function of either manufacturing, sales, or wholesaling. Initial growth was simple *volume expansion,* but it created a need for an administrative office. Next, a *geographic expansion* strategy created multiple field units in the same function and industry but in different locations. Administrative problems of interunit coordination, specialization, and standardization arose, and the functional departmental office was created to handle these issues. During the 1800s, these issues were first confronted by the railroads, which were the innovators emulated by other industries. Today, the same issues are raised by branch banking.

The next stage in the historical development of growth consisted of the strategies that involved *vertical integration.* That is, successful business firms stayed in the same industry but acquired or created other functions. Manufacturing plants created their own warehouses and wholesaling operations and their own sales force. New administrative problems arose in the effort to balance the sequential movement of goods through the interdependent functions. This led to the development of forecasts, schedules, and capacity balancing techniques. Here, the innovators were the steel companies that integrated back to the mining operations.

The last strategy analyzed by Chandler was the one of product diversification. Firms moved into new industries to employ existing resources as primary markets declined. The new problems in this case centered on the appraisal and evaluation of product divisions and alternative investment proposals. Time had to be allowed for the strategic management of this capital allocation process. Figure

Figure 2.1   Strategies and Structure

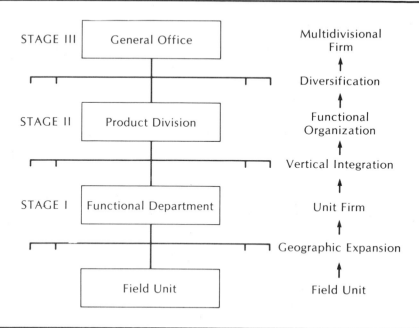

2.1 depicts all the strategies and the resulting structures that evolved, culminating in the multidivisional structure. This form, which created a division of labor based on a time horizon, was superior to the functional organization as a means of managing capital allocation in the face of diversity. The divisions were responsible for short-run operating decisions; the central office was responsible for strategic, long-run decisions. The office was to be staffed with general managers who were not responsible for short-run operating results and were thereby given the time and psychological commitment necessary for long-term planning in the interest of the corporation as a whole. There were enough general managers, usually group executives, to tie that strategic direction to internal control of divisional performance. However, there was not excessive management, which could often lead to local interference. In this way, the divisional form, which provided a balance of strategic direction and divisional autonomy, was superior to the functional organization and the holding company.

The first companies to create the multidivisional form were those that first experienced the effects of diversity. Du Pont and General Motors were the innovators this time. Their stories and those of

Sears Roebuck and Standard Oil make up the bulk of Chandler's book. He then traces the development of this new form throughout American enterprise. However, not all of the firms adopted the multidivisional form. The copper and aluminum companies, for example, did not. These were the companies that did not diversify product lines, however; they grew in one industry and supplied the same customers, employing strategies mentioned in Chapter 1 as those of single- and dominant-product businesses. Thus, these firms also demonstrate that structure follows strategy. Those firms that remained and grew within a single industry retained the centralized functional organization; those that diversified adopted the multidivisional structure. This strategy-structure linkage has been the part of Chandler's work that has been examined and reformulated most in subsequent studies. This point is not his only one, however.

A second part of Chandler's thesis is the hypothesis concerning the *stagewise development* of American enterprise. He argues, as has been summarized, that large American industrial enterprises began with a strategy of resource accumulation followed by a rationalization of its use through the functional organizational structure. Next came expansion into new markets through diversification, followed by the creation of the multidivisional structure in order to achieve a division of labor, based on a time horizon. Figure 2.1 represents these changes as shifts from Stage I through Stage III, to use the terms applied by Scott in subsequent works (Scott 1971, 1973). As Stage I organizations accumulated resources through vertical integration, they changed structures to the Stage II functional structure. After changing strategy to one of diversification, they changed structured again to the Stage III multidivisional form. This sequence was proposed as the stagewise development model of American enterprise. This model, too, has stimulated a good deal of subsequent study.

Although the last point to be discussed has not stimulated much subsequent empirical inquiry, it is becoming entrenched in current practice. Chandler found that the empire builder or the strategy formulator was rarely the individual who created the new structure to fit the new strategy. Those who acquired resources had professional backgrounds and interests different from those of the organizational innovators. One result of these divergent models of training and thought was that the entrepreneur rarely took time to do the logical thinking necessary for organizational analysis. As a result, the move from one stage of structure to another was a painful one. Only when economic inefficiency resulted and an entrepreneur left was the new structure created and put into place. Thus, the psychological difference between the entrepreneur and the organizer caused a delay between the formulation of strategy and implementation of structure, and the implementation of a new structure usually occurred only after severe provocation. Observation of this very phenomenon among high-growth, technology-based new ventures, which are increasingly prevalent, lends support to this point (Kazanjian 1983).

In summary, three main principles can be identified in Chandler's work:

- Organizational structure follows from the growth strategy pursued by the firm.
- American firms have followed a pattern of stagewise development from unifunctional structure, to the functional organization, to the multidivisional structure.
- The change from one stage to another occurred only after provocation, because the strategy formulator and the organizational innovator were different types of people.

In the following sections of the chapter, these points are reviewed together with empirical evidence created by subsequent research.

MARKETS AND HIERARCHIES: AN ECONOMIC PERSPECTIVE

The idea that strategy and structure are closely linked was picked up quickly by a number of different disciplines. In business schools, the business policy, organizational behavior, and management groups all incorporated it into their literature. Much subsequent empirical work has come from these sources.

In addition, other disciplines with an interest in organizational theory have adopted it to confirm some of their ideas, making some conceptual elaborations and extensions. For example, James D. Thompson (1967), a sociologist interested in organizations, utilized a similar framework in his interpretation of how organizations both shape and are shaped by their environments. He argued that the type and degree of interdependence between the organization and its environment are what define the firms' strategic choices, and he used much of Chandler's work to support specific propositions for organizational growth. (A fuller discussion of the relation of Thompson's work to issues of strategy and structure can be found in Galbraith and Nathanson [1978].)

Of more direct interest is work conducted by economists. Oliver Williamson (1970, 1975, 1979), a leading theorist in the growing field of institutional economics, has made an extensive study of structure. The primary focus of his research is on transaction costs, which has led him and others to examine different institutional arrangements for conducting economic activity. In the past, economists have been primarily preoccupied with prices and markets as the only institutions through which efficient economic transactions could take place. The institutionalists, however, see markets and firms as alternative institutions through which to conduct economic transactions. The firm should then choose the form that is more efficient or provides the lesser cost vehicle for the conduct of economic activity.

Williamson makes an argument that is obvious to business policy and organization theorists but not necessarily to economists: Internal organization makes an economic difference. Therefore, economists should be as concerned with internal organization structure as they are with market structure. Specifically, he suggests that when there are exchange circumstances characterized by uncertainty, and by idiosyncratic knowledge, small numbers, and opportunistic behavior, then market prices and market substitutes such as contracting are inefficient. Instead, it is more efficient to use an administrative process that takes an adaptive approach to uncertainty by making a sequence of decisions and transmitting the newly acquired information between the interested parties. He suggests that internal organization and administrative processes as we know them are the result of the aforementioned market failures. That is, under circumstances of uncertainty, of differentially distributed information, of opportunism, and of small numbers of participants, the invisible hand fails to do its job of clearing markets in an economically efficient manner. An inventor of an institutional form to replace the defective market can reap the benefits of increased economic efficiency. Such is the case with vertically integrated work flows managed through functional organizations instead of bilateral monopoly bargaining. Such is also the case with diversified businesses managed through the multidivisional structure, rather than by a capital market allocating funds to single-business functional organizations.

Williamson's view of the multidivisional firm as a miniature capital market is an interesting one. He sees the multidivisional form as a response to the inability of both functional organizations and capital markets to regulate decision-making discretion in organizations following both a substantial separation of management and ownership and an increase in a firm's size and complexity.

A search for substitute external controls has been set in motion on this account: solemn supplications on behalf of corporated responsibility have also been advanced. But the possibility that discretionary outcomes might be checked by reorganizational changes within the firm has been generally neglected. I submit, however, that organization innovations, which in the 1930's were just getting underway, have mitigated capital market failures by transferring functions traditionally imputed to the capital market to the firm instead. Not only were the direct effects of substituting internal organization for the capital market beneficial, but the indirect effects served to renew the efficacy of capital market controls as well. (Williamson 1975, 136)

Williamson argues that for large firms operating in diverse businesses, the multidivisional structure (M-form) is a more effective means of allocating capital in order to maximize profit than either the functional organization, the holding company, or businesses operating as independent units regulated only by product and capital markets. The argument proposed here against the functional organization is similar to Chandler's and to Berg's empirical work (Berg 1965). As a result of an insufficient number of general managers, the organization is unable to separate short-term operating decisions from long-term strategic decisions. The divisional form produces optimal allocation more often than individual units operating independently, because the incentive machinery of the organization creates greater goal compatibility between divisions and corporate management than that existing between owners and managers. In addition, management is better informed than investors because of information systems and more thorough audits, and because they allocate capital across divisions from low- to high-yield divisions with less cost than the capital market. The divisional form is superior to the holding company as well. Although the holding company can allocate cash flows from low- to high-yield divisions, it lacks the information and management necessary for strategic planning and internal control. As Williamson argues, "if indeed the firm is to serve effectively as a miniature capital market, which in many respects is what the M-form structure ought to be regarded, a more extensive internal control apparatus than the holding company form of organization possesses is required" (1975, 145).

Thus, for diversified businesses, the economic performance of the multidivisional form is usually higher than that of the functional organization, the holding company, and the operation of the divisions as independent companies. The comparison with holding companies is useful because it demonstrates that merely converting to a divisional form is not enough. Conversion must be accompanied by strategic direction, by internal incentives and controls, and by a management style that delegates short-run operation to the divisions. This package of structure, strategy, and process is a concept to which we shall return. Thus, the theoretical dimension of Williamson's work permits greater rigorous analyses of the implications of Chandler's initial findings.

EMPIRICAL RESEARCH

A considerable body of research has been stimulated directly by the works of Chandler and Williamson. From the early to the mid-1970s, research conducted through the Industrial Development and Public Policy Program at the Harvard Business School contributed several refinements and extensions of Chandler's thesis, which are summarized in the sections to follow. The work of Williamson in addition to that of Chandler has led to research on strategy-structure-performance linkages, which will be addressed in Chapter 3.

Extensions of Chandler

The first study in this program of research refined the concept of diversification and compared the strategies with regard to structural form (Wrigley 1970). Taking a sample from the Fortune 500, Wrigley distinguished four different strategies that were being followed. Some firms, such as the previously mentioned copper companies, stayed in a single-product business. Another group diversified but still had a single dominant business that accounted for 70 to 95 percent of sales. An example of single dominant-product business is the automobile industry. Still another group diversified but had more than 30 percent of their sales outside their main business in related businesses. The relation would be a common customer, a common distribution channel, or a common technology, for example. In any case, some connection existed among the products or businesses. Finally, the last group diversified into completely unrelated businesses and had more than 30 percent of their sales outside the main business. In matching structures to these strategies, Wrigley found that the more diversified the strategy, the more likely one is to find the multidivisional structure. Wrigley observed a hybrid form of structure also in use in the dominant business category. This group managed the dominant business through a functional structure and the diverse products through a divisionalized structure. This amounts to a partial move toward the multidivisional structure. Those companies that diversified into related and unrelated businesses overwhelmingly chose multidivisional structures. These results support the thesis that structure follows strategy in general, and that diversification leads to multidivisional forms in particular.

The same type of analysis was replicated for firms in the United Kingdom (Channon 1973) and France (Pooley-Dyas 1972). If structure follows strategy in the United States, why not in Europe also? The results, which show some similarities and differences, indicated that for all countries there is an increase in the amount of diversification between 1950 and 1970. Single- and dominant-business categories are substantial but declining. Similarly, there is an increase in the use of the multidivisional structure at the expense of functional and holding company alternatives. However. there are variations across countries, and in all cases the diversification strategy is more extensive than the multidivisional structure. The explanation offered is that diversification alone is not sufficient to bring about a reorganization of the power structure. It must be matched with competitive pressures. This is why the United Kingdom has gone further in implementing the multidivisional structure than its continental neighbors. The decline of tariff barriers in the Common Market is now causing competition on the continent, however.

The role of competition also emerged as a factor in a more recent study that tracked the strategy and structure of the top one hundred Japanese firms, also for the period from 1950 to 1970 and in a direct comparison with the study of U.K. firms previously cited (Suzuki 1980). The finding was that Japanese firms, despite their smaller size, diversified earlier, partly because of a smaller domestic market. Further observed was that a larger time gap was present between diversification and the adoption of a multidivisional structure. Such delays were hypothesized to result from several factors. First, government policy encouraged export, limited imports, and pushed firms to rationalize industries. Second, companies included in the study had historically been clustered into groups built around a major bank. Coordination of companies within groups took place to avoid internal competition. Last, some firms pursued diversification through associated and affiliated companies that were not completely owned.

Therefore it is evident that competition plays a role in the adoption of a multidivisional structure by diversified firms. Along with competition comes the multidivisional structure. Scott suggests that "the divisional structure appears to be the most effective way to manage the strategy of diversification under highly competitive conditions" (Scott 1973, 141). This view comes close to Williamson's idea that the divisional structure performs competitive capital market functions effectively.

The most comprehensive example of this research is the study by Rumelt (1974). He further elaborated the types of strategies of diversification. Through the use of subjective judgments and some quantitative measures, he created nine different strategies to characterize a sample of U.S. firms from the Fortune 500. The single-business category remained as defined previously, but the other three categories were elaborated.

The dominant-product business (in which sales associated with the dominant business account for 70 to 95 percent of total sales) was divided into four subcategories. The first subcategory was vertically integrated firms. These firms were classed as having sales outside the dominant business, but the products sold were by-products taken out of the sequential flow between stages of production. This strategy was different from those strategies involving independent businesses. The second, third, and fourth categories also apply as subclasses of the related business category. They characterize the degree of relatedness of the business into which the firm diversified. Some stayed "close to home" by adopting only products that utilized a common technology or market channel. These firms were classed as dominant-constrained. That is, their diversification was constrained by the desire to exploit a particular advantage. The next type was a firm that diversified in a manner that maintained links between businesses but was not constrained by one unifying link. That is, some products shared a common technology. Some of the technology sharers also shared a common distribution channel with another group of businesses. Viewed as a whole, the businesses appear unrelated, but links of varying types are between all of them. This category was called dominant-linked. The last category was simply dominant-unrelated; it characterized firms diversifying into business totally unrelated to the dominant and other businesses.

The related category, as just suggested, was divided into related-constrained and related-linked. The unrelated category was also subdivided into two types. The purpose was to create a separate category for the acquisitive conglomerate. The unrelateds were thus typed on the basis of their aggressiveness in acquiring other firms. This classification led to categories for the unrelated-passive and the acquisitive conglomerate, and made nine categories in all.

These strategies were then related to the type of structure. Rumelt classed structures as being functional, functional with subsidiaries, multidivisional (both product and geographic divisions), and holding companies, the last being a divisional structure characterized by highly autonomous divisions with a miniscule formal organization above them. Strategies and structures employed by the Fortune 500 were examined from 1949 to 1969.

The results for strategies demonstrate the decline of the single- and dominant-business categories over the twenty-year period, with single-business firms dropping from 42 percent in 1949 to 15 percent in 1969. Over the same time period, however, strategies of diversity were increasingly employed, with related diversified firms moving from 26 to 41 percent and unrelated diversified firms increasing from 4 to 19 percent.

In a subsequent study, Rumelt (1982) replicated the categorization of firms using a slightly modified scheme. (Dominant-linked and dominant-unrelated categories were combined, as were the acquisitive conglomerate and unrelated-passive categories). Covering the period from 1949 to 1974, his findings largely paralleled those of his earlier study. Therefore, it has been well substantiated that the pattern of American business during the 1950s, 1960s, and into the 1970s was toward a strategy of product diversification.

Regarding structure, Rumelt found that the multidivisional firm follows the diversification strategy as Chandler had predicted. Covering the same time period, the functional structures among Fortune 500 firms decreased from 63 percent in 1949 to only 11 percent by 1969, while the multidivisional firm increased from 20 to 76 percent. When strategy and structure were looked at together, Chandler's thesis was again supported. The single- and dominant-business strategies are conducted through functional organizations. The greater the diversity, the more likely one is to find the multidivisional firm. Over time, then, the relation between strategy and structure was observed to come into line, presumably because of competitive pressures in the market.

International Studies

A related program of research, the Harvard International Project (Fouraker and Stopford 1968; Stopford 1968; Stopford and Wells 1972; Franko 1974, 1976), has also generated a good deal of empirical study relevant to strategy and structure linkages. This group has followed the changes in structure that have accompanied strategies of international expansion of both U.S.- and European-based firms.

Stopford studied a sample of U.S. firms taken from the Fortune 500 as they expanded in the 1960s. In so doing, he found that American firms adopted common structures when following common strategies. The first major structural change adopted by these firms was the establishment of an international division that was added to the existing product divisionalized structure. However, the international division was a transitory form and gave way to another, more global form. Which global form a company moved to depended on the firm's international growth strategy. Those firms that took their entire diversified domestic product line abroad eventually adopted worldwide product divisions. Those firms that expanded internationally with only their dominant business adopted geographic divisions that divided the world into areas. Each of these strategies set up forces that led to the abandonment of the international division.

Franko (1974, 1976) conducted the same study examining the experience of European firms taken from the Fortune 200 of European companies along the same period. His initial findings did not support the Chandler thesis. The vast majority of European multinationals in 1961 were organized around an international holding company/domestic functional model. This form was used even when the multinationals pursued product diversification. However, this result was attributed to several factors, not the least of which was the existence of agreements and cartels that limited competitive pressures. Interestingly, by the early 1970s many of the firms in his sample shifted to the multidivisional structure.

Although these shifts differed by country and by industry, it can be generalized that as competition markedly increased with the reduction of tariff barriers to zero in the Common Market and with the entrance of both American and Japanese firms into local markets, more firms adopted multidivisional forms of organization. Franko concluded, then, that the greater the penetration by outside competitors and the greater the amount of antitrust activity, the more likely one is to find a move toward the multidivisional structure.

Thus, country and industry comparisons add further support to the case that diversity combined with competition leads to the multidivisional form. Neither alone is sufficient to provoke a change to the new structure. The European data analyzed by the Harvard group and by Franko extend the Chandler thesis to account for the competitive environment in which the strategy and structure linkage takes place. Structure apparently follows strategy only when structure makes a difference. When diversifying under monopoly conditions, however, strategy can be implemented independent of structure. The status quo offers the solution with the least resistance. Only when competition causes performance deterioration is structural adjustment needed to restore profits to acceptable levels.

This research, most directly represented by Rumelt's work, demonstrates the trend toward diversification by large firms in the Western world and the continuing adoption of the multidivisional form to manage that diversity. The international studies extend the range of observations over some new strategies and into new national contexts. In general, the results support the earlier suggestion about the importance of competition. Both diversification and competitive markets are needed to provoke a major structural change.

Collectively, however, the studies leave us hypothesizing about the relations between strategy, structure, economic performance, and competitiveness of markets. The empirical evidence just presented certainly supports the hypothesis that strategy and structure are related. But it has not yet been demonstrated that structure contributes to economic performance or that firms that have matched strategy and structure perform better than those that have not. For example, more recent research suggests that eventual positioning within a worldwide product organization, a geographic structure, or a product-area matrix may not be the ultimate strategy-structure fit. In a study of eighty-five multinational corporations, Davidson and Haspeslaugh (1982) found that from the period 1970 to 1980, those with a global product structure had the lowest increase in foreign sales when compared with firms using a matrix form. Interestingly, companies structured with operations grouped under an international division had the highest increase in foreign sales.

In a study of eleven large multibusiness, multinational companies (MNCs), Prahalad and Doz (1981) conclude that structure is not the sole factor in the long-run effectiveness of multinational enterprises. They argue that the strategic control of overseas subsidiaries by the head office of NMCs erodes over time due to the changing patterns of global competition, host government demands, and more complex business arrangements (such as joint ventures). Their findings suggest that "few MNCs have the privilege of adopting the simple strategic postures that a pure 'area' or 'product' mode indicates" (1981, 9). They argue, therefore, that the head office, working from a hybrid or a matrix structure, must use other mechanisms to influence behavior. These include (1) data management systems—accounting, planning, budgeting, and MIS; (2) manager management mechanisms—management placement, compensation, development, career progression, and performance evaluation; and (3) conflict resolution mechanisms—task forces, planning committees, integrative roles, and decision responsibility assignments.

Bartlett (1983) came to similar conclusions. In his own study of ten multinationals, he found that successful MNCs avoid a tendency to reorganize in the face of problems, but instead manage the complexity of geographic and market diversity through upgraded personnel, altered management systems, and multidimensional decision-making processes. The conclusions of both of these studies are consistent with our overall framework and with our earlier observation that organization is more than just structure. The implications of these findings are developed further in Chapter 9. The next chapter reviews those studies that have explicitly related structure, or strategy and structure, to financial performance.

SUMMARY AND MANAGERIAL IMPLICATIONS

This chapter has introduced the conceptual framework of strategy and structure, specifically through the works of Chandler and Williamson. Chandler suggests that as organizations change their growth strategy, new administrative problems arise that are solved when the organizational structure is refashioned to fit the new strategy. This redesigning is necessary, because each structure facilitates a certain set of processes that must also fit the product-market strategy being pursued. The theoreticians suggest, then, that alternative organizational forms make an economic difference.

The functional structure is seen as sufficient for providing the interunit coordination, specialization, and standardization needed to run an organization that has a single or dominant product-market strategy. This structure represents the first and second step in Chandler's stagewise development of the firm. The multidivisional structure, an improved form for dealing with diversity, represents the third stage in an organization's growth. It is an attempt to deal with the critical interdependencies that by necessity emerge across related businesses. Decentralization of authority and responsibility allows for decision making at lower levels in the hierarchy. Almost all the resources needed to do a job are placed at the division's disposal. This structure permits quicker response to individual market demands by reducing the need for communication and information processing. It also facilitates the capital allocation process by providing clear-cut appraisals and evaluations of both divisional performance and alternative investment proposals.

Viewed by Williamson as a miniature capital market, the multidivisional structure is superior to both the functional and the holding company forms. The functional organization, which provides too few general managers, results in the inability to separate long-term strategic decisions from short-term operating decisions. The multidivisional structure, however, creates a division of labor based on time horizon, enabling divisions to concentrate on short-run operating decisions while the central office focuses upon strategic long-run decisions.

The holding company is viewed as being similar to the external capital market because it is decentralized to the point where the central office makes decisions solely on the basis of financial performance. However, Williamson argues it is not as efficient as the M-form in this regard, given its lack of internal administrative and control mechanisms.

Based upon empirical research, general support is found for Chandler's major thesis that organizational structure follows its growth strategy. However, one refinement to this theory concerns the explication of competition as an important variable. Studies conducted in Europe and Japan indicated that diversification strategies outnumbered multidivisional structures. Apparently, diversification must also be matched by competitive pressures in order for the thesis to hold.

Rumelt has conducted comprehensive studies that categorized nine different types of diversification strategies while also classifying structures as functional, functional with subsidiaries, multidivisional, and holding company. The results showed the decline of the single and dominant product-market strategies over a twenty-five-year period, and also illustrated how the functional and holding company forms had given way to the multidivisional structure.

From this data, it may appear that the strategy-structure match should be pursued to achieve a high level of performance. That is, single- or dominant- business firms should be organized functionally, related diversified firms should have a multidivisional structure, and unrelated diversified firms should be organized as a holding company. Although such a match describes what firms have done for the reasons discussed previously, it is not clear that the strategy and structure match per se will lead to effective performance. We shall reserve any prescriptive guidance until the issue of performance has been examined in considerable detail in Chapter 3.

3

Strategy, Structure, and Performance

Throughout Chapter 2, the implicit assumption was that to be economically effective, strategy and structure must be matched. The fact that under competitive conditions few mismatches occur is taken as evidence supporting the assumption. Although the nonexistence of mismatches supports this premise, it does not eliminate alternative explanations. One can also point to some, albeit few, mismatches that do exist. Further, if a relation exists but its magnitude is small, then managers should concentrate on other factors to improve performance.

As will be seen in this chapter, strategy, structure, external contingencies (such as environment and technology), and market structure have all—singly and in various combinations—been theorized to influence the economic performance of the firm, either directly or as a result of the attainment of a fit among variables. A simplified version of the primary relationships posited in these research streams, to be reviewed in the sections that follow, is shown in Figure 3.1.

CONTINGENCY THEORY AND PERFORMANCE

Some of the earliest studies that focused on assessing firm performance can be found in the field of organization theory. A portion of this work, known as contingency theory, is relevant to considerations of strategy and structure. The conceptual foundation of this view is built upon empirical research that investigates the role of technology, environment, and size upon organizational structure. The initial impetus came from British sociologists and organization theorists.

*Figure 3.1   Research Variables Related
to the Economic Performance of the Firm*

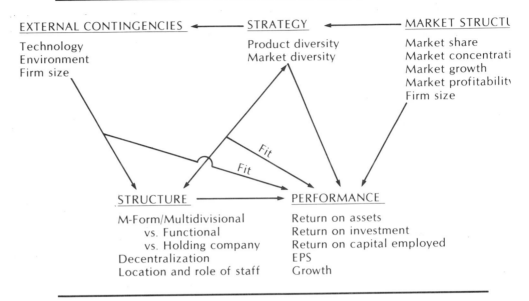

Joan Woodward (1965) proposed that manufacturing technology was a prime determinant of organizational form. Subsequent research has substantiated parts of her original findings (Gerwin 1979). However, another later wave of research suggests that much of the impact of technology is more accurately attributed to size, especially in large firms (Blau and Schoenherr 1971; Hinings and Lee 1971; Child and Mansfield 1972). (For a recent review of this literature and its various findings, see Fry [1982].) But, as such research generally centers on the manufacturing function and lower-level structural constructs, this school of thought is not of primary concern.

Burns and Stalker (1961), two other British sociologists, suggested that the rate of environmental change was what determined organizational form. They suggested that in industries characterized by high rates of change in markets and technology, successful firms adopted an "organic form." Such an organization was decentralized with ambiguous roles and a great deal of lateral communication. In industries with stable markets and product lines, Burns and Stalker proposed that successful firms adopted a mechanistic organization, characterized by centralization and well-defined roles, with communication following the chain of command. Thus, according to this perspective, the type of organization (structure) is contingent upon the rate of environmental change (strategy). For example, those firms in high-technology industries and in markets characterized by rapid change, given strategies of new product introduction, should adopt decentralized, organic forms.

Building upon Burns and Stalker's work, Lawrence and Lorsch (1967) more fully established the rationale for contingency theory with the publication of *Organization and Environment.* Examining ten firms in three industries, they showed that high-performing firms in an uncertain environment had greater decentralization than low performers and that in industries with more predictable environments, the high performers were more centralized. All high performers had achieved a fit with their environments. The addition of performance as an outcome variable strengthened the credibility of contingency theory. Subsequently, a number of other studies followed that included performance measures.

In addition to the contingency perspectives relating technology and environment to structure and performance, a third major research track emerged, which ultimately viewed structure as resulting primarily from increases in size. Influenced heavily by the seminal work of Weber (1947) and best represented by the work of the Aston group (Pugh, Hickson, Hinings, Macdonald, Turner, and Lupton 1963, 1968, 1969), this research examined the role of contextual variables (size, ownership, location, and technology) on the underlying bureaucratic dimensions of structure: formalization, centralization, specialization, and standardization. (Note that the level and nature of organizational structure in these studies are not directly comparable to the more macrolevel types of Chandler and Williamson. However, the two are consistent.)

Child (1974, 1975) extended these studies to examine structure and performance. He was interested in the effects of size and dynamic environments on the degree to which firms acquired formal controls and staff specialists, and delegated authority. Increases in each are referred to as the degree of bureaucratization. The high-performing firms acquired bureaucracy at a faster rate when they grew than did the poor performers. With size should come bureaucracy. Although the high performers in dynamic environments acquired bureaucracy at a slower rate than the high performers in stable industries, they did so faster than low performers in both environments. In a dynamic environment, a balance must be struck between bureaucracy for size and responsiveness for change. Again, the notion is one of fit.

Contingency theory has relevance for strategy implementation. However, instead of focusing upon strategy, these studies have considered various factors that influence the tasks to be performed by the firm. Accordingly, structure should vary with task uncertainty (a product of environment). This is consistent with Chandler's view, because uncertainty and diversity tend to covary and diversity is, in part, a product of strategy (diversification). The influence of size is also consistent with Chandler, as he views strategy as growth driven.

Nonetheless, the general nature of these studies and their early interpretation were deterministic. Structure was largely seen by organization theorists as the result of these situational variables with little role for intervening factors. Child (1972) challenged this view, doing so in part through references to Chandler and thereby establishing a direct link to the strategy-structure literature. He argued that research built upon static, statistically established associations (as was the case with much of contingency theory) elaborates nothing of the underlying processes by which they resulted. Further, he proposed that strategic choice on the part of top managers is a critical variable that directly influences organization through the selection of environments (product-market positions) in which the firm places itself and of the goals and performance levels to be pursued. Further, he suggested that firms can indeed influence their environments through a range of competitive actions. This incorporation of strategy as a contingency factor has been increasingly accepted and adopted by organization theorists. Recent research (Grinyer and Yasai-Ardekani 1980, 1981) has investigated bureaucratic structural characteristics of the Chandler structural types, representing extensions to both streams of research.

Although studies can be found that do not support the fit hypothesis (Mohr 1971; Pennings 1975), the majority of the contingency work, including that reviewed previously, supports the importance of attaining a fit between strategy and structure. However, several problems remain within this literature. First is the issue of causation. As mentioned by Child, it is not clear from studies such as these whether, for example, centralization causes low performance or vice versa. Second, although structure and performance appear to be related, the strength of that relationship is unclear from this research.

STRATEGY, STRUCTURE, AND PERFORMANCE

In the study discussed in Chapter 2, Rumelt (1974) also examined the financial performance of the firms in the sample in order to test strategy-structure-performance relations. First, economic performance and type of strategy were compared. The finding was that the type of diversification, not the amount, was related to economic performance. Both constrained strategies, dominant and related, were the top performers in almost all categories such as return on equity, stability, and various categories of growth. Thus, a strategy of controlled diversity is associated with high stable economic performance, because it neither commits the organization to a single business nor stretches it across industries. Instead, controlled diversity reflects the reason for the entry into related businesses: that all may draw upon a common strength or a distinctive competence. However, controlled diversity may not necessarily be the cause of economic performance; it may also result from it. The low-performing related-constrained types may leave to try related-linked businesses, leaving the high-performing related-constrained firms. Cause and effect statements cannot be made yet.

The multidivisional structure per se was the high performer in all growth areas and in risk-adjusted growth in earnings per share. It had average return on equity and capital. This finding is interesting, because growth is often assumed to be purchased at the expense of reduced profitability. Instead, growth and profitability were positively related, and the multidivisional firms were able to increase profits faster than functional organizations while maintaining the same return on capital. The reason is assumed to be the planning, control, and reward systems used in multidivisional structures:

> Unlike many functionally organized firms, and particularly unlike a vertically integrated firm, the diversified divisionalized company does not have to reinvest in marginal activities just to "stay in the game"; its strategy permits, and its structure facilitates, a range of policies tailored to individual businesses. Some areas can be used as cash generators or dropped entirely; others may provide stable long term performance and still others may consist of risky, but potentially lucrative new ventures. As a result, there is less conflict on the corporate level between the goals of profitability and growth. (Rumelt 1974, 126)

Again, it is not only the divisional structure but also the matching of processes and systems to strategy, as well as to the achievement of short-run profit in the divisions and long-term growth overall, that is important.

Rumelt's second test controlled for strategy. Within the related strategies (constrained and linked), Rumelt hypothesized that the multidivisionals would outperform the functional organization. Partial support for this proposition was found. Return on equity, return on capital, and price-earnings ratios were higher, but they were not statistically significant. Growth in earnings per share, which was higher for functional organizations, was also not statistically significant. The only significant difference was that multidivisionals produced higher sales growth. Four out of five hypotheses were therefore in the predicted direction, and one was significant. However, no attempt was made to analyze variance to determine the relative contribution of strategy, structure, or fit. This evidence is supportive but not overwhelming.

In summary, then, Rumelt found that success could result from pursuing good strategies, from adopting a good structure, or from creating a match between the two. Recall that he found that strategies resulted in varying degrees of success, with the related businesses performing best. The multidivisional structure was the best performer for growth and had average returns on equity and capital. Growth and returns were also positively related, showing that the multidivisional structure could achieve growth without sacrificing profitability.

Parts of the Rumelt research have been replicated by Channon in a study of British service industry firms such as banks, insurance companies, and hotels (1977). Using the categories of single business, dominant business, diversification into related businesses, and diversification into unrelated businesses, Channon found that the single-business and related business categories were superior on a number of measures of growth and returns, with the related businesses being marginally superior overall. This finding suggests that diversification is pursued only after the single business begins to decline. If prospects are good, no diversification occurs. When diversification does occur, however, greater success is achieved by going into related businesses as opposed to unrelated ones.

Channon's structure results were somewhat similar to Rumelt's. The multidivisional firms had high growth results for sales, assets, and earnings per share while maintaining above-average returns. The functional organizations had slightly higher returns, and holding companies were the poorest performers. Unfortunately, no test was made for the fit between strategy and structure.

Another study tested the effects of using a profit center structure (presumably a multidivisional) versus not using one (presumably a functional organization) (Poensgen 1974). Using financial data taken from Compustat tapes and structure categories from a questionnaire (Mauriel and Anthony 1966), correlations, with controls for factors such as size and industry, were computed for 364 American firms. The result shows that profit center structures are more profitable, with structure explaining about 10 percent of the variance in return on equity. This is one of the few measures of importance and indicates that structure can have an effect of up to 10 percent. Cause and effect analysis yielded no results. Before and after data did not show an increase in profitability after going to the profit center structure. Finally, Rumelt's results of low association between returns and growth for profit centers were reproduced. Presumably, with one group working on returns (divisions) and one group working on growth (corporate), the association between the two is less. Growth in a multidivisional structure does not depend on profit from current operations to the degree that it does in a functional organization.

More recent studies have attempted to replicate Rumelt's study and findings. With a sample of eighty firms, Bettis (1981) found that related diversified firms outperformed unrelated diversified firms on return on assets by as much as 3 percent, linking the result to synergistic effects from advertising and research and development. This finding reinforced that of Rumelt. However, another study by Bettis and Hall (1982) found no significant performance difference between firms pursuing the related-constrained and the related-linked strategies. Finally, they suggested that some of the performance differences between categories of related and unrelated diversification were attributable to the number of firms drawn from a single highly profitable industry (pharmaceuticals).

Focusing more directly on strategy, structure, and performance linkages, but utilizing a different, more detailed strategic categorization scheme from those referenced previously, Nathanson (1980; Nathanson and Cassano 1982) found that structure significantly affected performance in a study of 206 U.S. firms. Nathanson categorized firms according to both product diversity and market diversity (see Table 3.1) to capture strategy. Measuring performance in terms of return on capital employed (ROCE) and controlling for size (smaller firms were defined as having less than $225 million in sales; larger were defined as having more than that), they found:

> Smaller firms do well relative to larger firms in categories marked by no diversification and in categories of extremely high diversification. Larger firms do significantly better than smaller firms in the in-between categories—those characterized by intermediate levels of diversification. (Nathanson and Cassano 1982, 24)

These findings resulting from the inclusion of size represent a meaningful contribution.

The importance of the strategy-structure fit can be seen by examining performance differences found across the categories of product diversity. Within the Single Nexus category, among smaller firms the functional organizations significantly outperformed the multidivisionals, as would be expected. Interestingly, for larger firms, this structural distinction had no effect on performance.

Employing a more detailed definition of structure, performance

Table 3.1   Nathanson's Product and Market Diversity Categories

Product Diversity Categories	Market Diversity Categories
Single Nexus (SN) Essentially one product or product line *Examples:* Wrigley, Schlitz, Maytag	Single-Business Group (SBG) Essentially one business market *Examples:* Wrigley, Schlitz
Highly Related Nexus (HRN) Majority of business in one product or product line *Examples:* Caterpillar Tractor, Merck, McGraw-Hill, Xerox	Highly Related Business Group (HRBG) Majority of business ($\geq$ 70%) in one business market *Examples:* Tonka, Valmont, Oil, Steel
Related Nexus (RN) Majority of business related by either raw materials, engineering, or technology *Examples:* Gardner Denver, McQuay Perfex, International Harvester	Related Business Group (RBG) Majority of business ($\geq$ 60%) in one business market or general industry *Examples:* Clark, General Foods, Memorex
Diversified Nexus (DN) Majority of business accounted for by unrelated products but engaged in no more than seven unrelated areas *Examples:* Air Products, Tenneco	Diversified Business Group (DBG) Two to four unrelated business markets *Examples:* Moog, Nashua, Air Products Highly Diversified Business Group (HDBG) Five to six unrelated business markets *Examples:* Ingersoll-Rand, Excello, Illinois Tool Works
Unrelated Nexus (UN) Majority of business accounted for by unrelated products with at least eight unrelated areas *Examples:* Gulf & Western, Northwest Industries, Rockwell International	Unrelated Business Group (UBG) Seven or more unrelated business markets *Examples:* Dow, Gulf & Western, GE, Olin

Source: Nathanson and Cassano (1982), 22.

differences found among firms within the Highly Related Nexus were also attributed to organization. Specifically, those firms demonstrating characteristics of top-down planning and overly strong coordination activities, whether functional or multidivisional, registered the lowest performance rating in the sample (ROCE of 8.0), while multidivisional firms within this group not demonstrating those characteristics had an average ROCE of 13.4. Interestingly, smaller firms were more likely to be in the former category than in the latter.

For Related Nexus firms, the location and role of staff was a factor: "Findings indicate that it is important to have a strong staff at the group level while not having too much staff at the divisional level. This structure enables these firms to take best advantage of the relatedness of products" (Nathanson and Cassano 1982, 26). Performance declined as the strength of group staff declined. Those firms with highly autonomous divisions in this category are significantly the poorest performers. Here again, small firms in this category fared poorly, possibly due to resource constraints that limited staffing options.

The reverse was the case for more diversified firms (Diversified Nexus). Here, successful firms demonstrated superior performance when corporate staff was minimal and divisional self-containment was high. Further, performance deteriorates as the size and power of group-level staff increase. Overall, Nathanson's findings, offering some new and different perspectives, are an interesting contrast to the studies cited previously.

DIVERSITY, DECENTRALIZATION, AND PERFORMANCE

Many of the studies cited in this and later sections focus on the structural dimension of decentralization. This dimension was implicit in many of the aforementioned studies. Chandler spoke of the centralized functional organization and the decentralized multidivisional form. However, within any multidivisional form is the choice of the extent of divisional autonomy that is appropriate for the implementation of strategy. Several studies have directly addressed the question of autonomy and strategy.

Berg (1965) addressed the question of structural differences in explaining why the conglomerates of the 1960s were effective. He noted two types of divisional structures: the conglomerate and the diversified majors. The diversified majors, which were the multidivisional type of form described by Chandler, usually had several hundred people in the corporate office. They coordinated divisional activity through corporate policies and direct participation of corporate offices. In contrast, the conglomerate, similar to the holding company, would have ten to twenty general managers with specialists only in the tax, legal, and financial areas. The conglomerate, then, placed nearly all functions within the division and eliminated the need for coordination. Corporate divisional interests were coordinated through the reward system.

The greater decentralization in the conglomerate case was justified because they managed greater diversity. Berg describes them as diversifying into unrelated businesses, to use Rumelt's categories. The diversified majors were less diverse and followed a strategy of diversifying into related businesses. The relatedness of these divisions required some coordination in the corporate interest, thereby necessitating more corporate management. Thus, greater diversity of a quantitative and qualitative nature requires greater divisional autonomy and smaller corporate offices.

A second study that addresses the issue is based on an empirical study of six divisional firms (Lorsch and Allen 1973). The firms varied in the degree of diversity, the degree of uncertainty, and the amount of interdivisional trading. Indeed, two firms had sufficient interdivisional transfers to be called vertically integrated. The other four firms were classed as conglomerates. Lorsch and Allen measured a number of dimensions of organization, some of which are dealt with more fully later on in this chapter. The concern here is with the size of the corporate offices, the functions performed at corporate offices, and the degree of divisional autonomy. Table 3.2 shows data relevant to the first two questions.

Three of the conglomerates fit the pattern suggested by Berg. They had small corporate offices and performed few divisional functions. The one conglomerate that operated as a vertically integrated firm was also the poorest performer. In contrast the vertically integrated units were larger, performed more corporate functions, and served in some operating as well as policy roles in these functions.

Lorsch and Allen also measured the amount of integrating efforts expended at corporate offices on corporate-divisional relations and interdivisional relations. The lower-performing vertically integrated firm was shown to spend too little effort in integrating the interdependent divisions. On the other hand, the lower-performing conglomerates were characterized by too much integrative effort.

These findings regarding diversity and organization were further reinforced by the recent work of Dundas and Richardson (1982). In their study of unrelated diversified firms, they found that successful firms pursuing such a strategy operated in what might be termed a holding company organization structure, with a small corporate office and largely autonomous operating divisions. This is because "central corporate functions such as marketing, research and development, and engineering are unnecessary because by definition the operating businesses are unrelated and consequently it is virtually impossible to establish functions such as these that are relevant to the firm as a whole" (Dundas and Richardson 1982, 296). Among the successful firms, finance and accounting, legal, acquisitions, and planning were the functions housed at the corporate office.

**Table 3.2   Basic Characteristics of
Corporate Headquarters Units in Six Firms**

	Conglomerate Firms			Vertically Integrated Firms		
	1	2	3	4	5	6
A. Size—total number of management and professional employees	17	20	25	230	479	250
B. Functions performed in Reference to divisions						
1. Financial-control	Xp	Xp	Xp	Xp	Xo,p	Xo,p
2. Long-range planning	Xp	Xp	Xp	Xp	Xo,p	Xo,p
3. Legal	Xo,p	Xo,p	Xo,p	Xo,p	Xo,p	Xo,p
4. Industrial relations	Xo,p	Xo,p	Xo,p	Xo,p	Xo,p	Xo,p
5. Operations research					Xp	
6. Marketing		Xp	Xp	Xo	Xo	Xo
7. Manufacturing/industrial engineering			Xp	Xp		
8. Planning and scheduling of output					Xo	Xo
9. Purchasing					Xo	Xo
10. Engineering (other than industrial)				Xp		
11. Research and development				Xo,p	Xo	Xo

Source: Jay W. Lorsch and Steven A. Allen III, *Managing Diversity and Interdependence: An Organizational Study of Multidivisional Firms.* Boston: Division of Research, Harvard Business School, 1973, p. 148. Reprinted by permission.

Note: An **X** indicates that certain functions in specified areas are performed by the headquarters unit for the divisions. A *p* indicates that corporate involvement is of a policy-setting nature (i.e., setting policies, advising, providing basic approaches). An *o* indicates an operating responsibility for the headquarters unit (e.g., actually carrying out some purchasing activities for certain divisions).

As required by size, group executives are used by these firms to facilitate span of control, ensure efficient capital allocation, and serve as an internal consultant. Typically, group executives in these situations have no staff reporting to them.

The conclusion from this last group of studies is that strategies characterized by diversity and uncertainty require greater decentralization and self-containment of divisions. When autonomy is not given, lower performance results. Strategies leading to interdivisional interdependence, such as vertical integration, require more corporate integrative effort. When too little autonomy is given, lower performance results. The extent of decentralization follows from the strategy.

THE M-FORM STRUCTURE AND PERFORMANCE: EXTENSIONS OF WILLIAMSON

Although similar to studies reviewed in the previous sections, the studies included within this section represent direct extensions of Williamson's work discussed in Chapter 2. Cable and Steer (1977) examined the economic performance of eighty-two British firms. The primary independent variable was optimal organizational form, operationalized in terms of the multidivisional form, with separation of division and corporate interests based on time horizon, and functional organizations in a single business. Nonoptimal forms were holding companies, multidivisionals with corporate offices too involved in division activities, and diversified functional forms. Controlling for size, industry, ownership, and growth, the authors found that organizational form is a significant predictor of return on equity and assets, accounting for between 7 and 9 percent difference in returns. Overall, the authors explain about 50 percent of the variance. Unfortunately, the criteria for determining the optimal organization are not explicit. However, the inclusion of several regressions with questionable cases omitted or reclassified produces little change in overall results. Some care should be taken in interpreting the authors' conclusion that organization makes a difference, as involvement by corporate superiors may be a response to, not a cause of, poor performance. The nonoptimal classification distorts the effect of organization. The results, like those of other correlation studies, should be interpreted cautiously with respect to causation.

Armour and Teece (1978) conducted a test of Williamson's M-form hypothesis based upon a sample of twenty-eight petroleum firms during the period from 1955 to 1973. They argue, based upon Williamson, that "an optimally organized M-form firm will realize superior performance not only because the resource conversion process is more efficient (i.e., the firm is operating closer to the production possibility frontier), but also because the strategic planning and decision making processes allocate resources to high-yield opportunities more effectively" (Armour and Teece 1978, 109).

They go on to suggest, though, that once the M-form, viewed as an organizational or administrative innovation, has diffused broadly across the industry, performance differences will no longer exist. Indeed, findings from their study support both hypotheses. For the period from 1955 to 1968, multidivisional forms realized a rate of return on stockholders' equity on average 2 percent higher than that realized by functionally organized firms. This finding was statistically significant. Results also indicate that observable superior multidivisional performance does not exist for the period from 1969 to 1973, a time by which the authors propose the M-form structure was fully diffused. They conclude, then, that the differential exists only as long as some firms have not adopted the appropriate form.

In a cross-industry study, Teece (1981) conducted another test of Williamson's M-form hypothesis. In this case, he selected matched pairs of firms in twenty industries. The first of each pair was identified as the first firm to adopt the M-form structure. Those firms were then matched with the leading competitor from their industry, typically the largest of the product-comparable firms, as a control. Using small sample statistics, Teece found that the early M-form adopters outperformed their competitors, but that the differential narrowed with time (and diffusion of the M-form within the industry), thus again supporting the hypothesis. In addition to these empirical works, Burton and Obel (1980) conducted a computer-simulated test of the M-form and also found support for it.

The two Teece studies should be recognized for having made a significant contribution to our understanding of the strategy-structure relationship, as they are two of the few direct tests of strategy-structure fit. Based upon the studies reviewed so far in this chapter, the strategy-structure fit is apparently of some significance. However, how much of the variance associated with performance can be attributed to fit remains unclear. Second, causal interpretations cannot be made from the correlational data upon which most of these studies are based. Teece's studies suggest, however, that the fit relationship is much more important when it serves as a competitive advantage utilized by a few leading-edge firms before diffusion and adoption across an industry. Nonetheless, as will be seen in the next section, performance differences may be attributable to other factors as well.

MARKET STRUCTURE AND PERFORMANCE

Much of the research reviewed so far appears to indicate that economic performance is determined by managerial choices of strategy and organization. As Christensen and Montgomery (1981) state:

> Rumelt's work has commonly been interpreted to mean that various diversification-profiles lead to varied performance levels. However, the correlational nature of Rumelt's results cannot support such con-

clusions, a caution Rumelt himself noted (1974:156). Beyond the difficulty of establishing causality scientifically, the linkage has not been examined rigorously for potential moderating or confounding effects. That is, rival explanations for the observed linkage have not been ruled out. In particular, research from industrial organization economics raises the possibility that market structure variables account for some or all of the differences Rumelt observed between strategy and corporate economic performance. (p. 328)

According to this view, the choice of product-market positions in which the firm competes could be the most important choice.

In their study of 128 firms, Christensen and Montgomery duplicated Rumelt's categorization (focusing on only six of the original nine categories). Interestingly, their classification for 125 of the 128 firms matched that of Rumelt's, with the remaining three requiring a classification change. This result strongly reinforces the reliability of this strategic classification scheme.

More importantly, however, this study tested the effect of market structure on performance. Specifically, it hypothesized that Rumelt's high-performance categories would be positioned in businesses with more favorable market characteristics. Market structure variables included market share, market concentration, market growth, market profitability, and absolute firm size.

Results suggest that significant differences of market structure variable measures did exist across strategic categories: "Two individual categories displayed interesting and significant differences. Unrelated portfolio firms were found to have lower market shares, to be positioned in less profitable and less concentrated markets and to be significantly smaller than other firms in the sample. Related constrained firms, on the other hand, were found to be more profitable, faster growing and in more highly concentrated markets than other firms" (Christensen and Montgomery 1981, 339).

These findings lead us to a potentially different interpretation of the findings of earlier research. As Figure 3.2 suggests, both firm performance and strategy may well be determined, in part, by market structure. That is, related-constrained diversified firms are successful because they operate in growing, highly concentrated, highly profitable markets while participating only in areas that utilize the firms' core strengths. Unrelated diversified firms do not perform well because they operate in fragmented, low-profitability markets. Citing the concept of defensive diversification, the authors postulate that firms that operated in low-growth, low-profit markets are the most likely candidates for diversification. Further, such firms are likely to find a similar lack of potential associated with markets that could be entered through constrained diversification, and hence would be more likely to pursue unrelated diversification. Interest-

Figure 3.2   Effects of Market Structure on Strategy and Performance

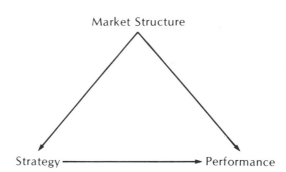

Adapted from Christensen, H. Kurt, and Cynthia A. Montgomery "Corporate Economic Performance: Diversification Strategy Versus Market Structure" *Strategic Management Journal,* 2 (1981): 327–43.

ingly, Dundas and Richardson (1982) found that the succesful unrelated diversified firms typically invest only in businesses that stand either first or second in their industries, thus reinforcing the importance of market structure variables.

Rumelt's current work (Rumelt and Wensley 1981; Lippman and Rumelt 1982; Rumelt 1982) picks up on this relationship between market structure and profitability, arguing that correlational relationships suggest nothing about causality. Further, he argues that both market share and profitability may be a factor of some other variable that resists precise identification and which he terms uncertain imitability. This term refers not to uncertainty of technology, sales, or production, but rather to "ambiguity as to what factors are responsible for superior (or inferior) performance [which] acts as a powerful block on both imitation and factor mobility.... The concept does not apply when differences in efficiency are rapidly diminished through imitation or factor mobility (e.g., non patentable inventions, copyable product ideas)" (Lippman and Rumelt 1982, 421).

SUMMARY AND MANAGERIAL IMPLICATIONS

This chapter has outlined empirical research, stimulated by the strategy-structure linkage, that investigates determinants of firm performance. Rumelt's performance data indicated that controlled diversity, which reflects businesses that all draw upon a common strength or distinctive competence, is the one associated with high stable economic performance. Similarly, the multidivisional structure is the high performer in almost all financial areas. The reason is assumed to be the planning, control, and reward system used in the multidivisional structure. The structure facilitates a range of policies tailored to individual businesses. Again, it is not just the divisional structure that is important, but also the matching of processes and systems to strategy. Rumelt failed, however, to show conclusively that the fit between strategy and structure was an important predictor of financial performance. The lack of findings in this area could have been caused by methodological problems concerning the nature of the sample and by the sample size. Other plausible explanations include a failure to look at the internal processes and at alternative mechanisms for coordination.

Nathanson and Cassano, employing a different scheme that categorized strategy according to both product and market diversity, found results generally consistent with those of Rumelt.

Teece, extending the work of Williamson, conducted several tests of the M-form hypothesis. His findings support directly the importance of a strategy-structure match to performance. Second, his results suggest that the strategy-structure match leads to high performance only as long as competitive firms in comparable situations have not attained such a fit. Once widely adopted within an industry, performance differences tended to diminish. Implicit in this finding is the notion that those firms that do not adopt the M-form innovation will have lower performance. (It should be noted that Teece's use of a single industry sample and of a matched pair research design controlled for market structure variables.)

Finally, Christensen and Montgomery have found that performance differences across categories of firms may not be attributable solely to the particular strategy (degree of diversity) or the strategy-structure match, but rather to market structure variables. Their results suggest that related diversified firms are positioned in markets that are growing, profitable, highly concentrated, and utilize the firms' core strengths. Unrelated diversified firms do not perform well in part because they operate in fragmented, low-profitability markets.

Taken comprehensively, these findings indicate the necessity to move toward a more integrative approach to understanding corporate financial performance. Strategy does make a difference in terms of the degree of diversity (related-unrelated diversification) pursued as well as the market structure characteristics of the specific product-market positions in which the firm places itself. The latter must be consistent with the core skills of the firm.

Second, the choice of strategy must be matched with an appropriate organizational form. Thus, strategy-structure fit is probably only one among several key linkages, including the strategy-environment (market structure) link. This assertion is consistent with the findings of Lenz (1981), who found that a comprehensive profile of consistency or fit among environment, strategy, and organization was associated with effective performance.

From these findings, several relevant guidelines emerge for managers regarding strategy and structure:

1. Performance is the product of multiple factors, but two are primary:
   a. Matching strategy to industry structure and core skills, (see Hofer and Schendel [1978] for detailed discussions of this issue); and
   b. Matching organizational structure to strategy.

2. Given a strategy that requires greater or lesser diversity, positioned in industrial settings characterized by favorable market structure variables, the firm must organize to match structure to the primary demands of strategy.
   a. *Single-business and dominant-business firms should be organized in a functional structure.* This allows for strong task focus through an emphasis on specialization and efficiency while providing the opportunity for adequate controls through centralized review and decision making. As Nathanson (1980) notes, this is particularly the case with smaller firms.
   b. *Related diversified firms should be organized into a multidivisional form.* Highly related businesses should be organized into groups within this form of structure. When synergies are possible within such groups, the appropriate location for staff influence and decision making is at the group level, with a lesser role for corporate-level staff. The greater the degree of diversity across businesses, the more the power of staff and decision-making authority should be decentralized within the divisions.
   c. *Unrelated diversified firms should be organized into a holding company structure.* Although this structure somewhat resembles a multidivisional structure, there are significant differences. With a holding company form, functions centralized and located at the corporate office should include finance, accounting, planning, legal, and related activities. As there are no synergies across businesses, the corporate office functions largely as a capital allocation and control mechanism. Beyond funds flows, major decisions involve choices of acquisition and divestiture. All operational matters are decentral-

ized to the individualized divisions. Group executives may be employed to reduce the span of control of the corporate office, but they typically have a minimum of staff, if any, and oversee each division discretely with no attempts at interdivisional activity.

d. *An early adoption of a strategy-structure fit can comprise a competitive advantage.* A performance advantage goes to the first firm among competitors to achieve an appropriate strategy-structure fit. Although this advantage will disappear as other firms attain such a fit, it is important to note that the loss of fit thereafter will lead to a competitive disadvantage to the firm. Alternatively, if the firm alters its strategy, its structure must obviously change as well.

As will be seen in subsequent chapters, however, structure is only one of a number of managerial variables that must be consciously designed in accordance with the strategy of the firm.

4

Implementing Diversification Strategies: An Alternative Framework

As the literature reviewed in Chapters 2 and 3 indicates, a considerable body of research has emerged in recent years that has advanced our knowledge of diversification. Through the work of Wrigley, Rumelt, and others, a range of diversification categories or strategies has been defined, and the relationship of firm diversity and performance has been explored. Rumelt's research clearly demonstrated that the Fortune 500 have moved dramatically toward diversified positions. Also, his findings and those of others indicate that a strategy of related diversification is correlated with high performance. And yet, little is known about which factors influence diversification and how to go about implementing a diversification once it has been decided upon. This chapter briefly reviews which conditions influence the choice of diversification by firms and what relatedness, a measure of diversification, means. We then propose an alternative framework for diversification and discuss its implications for implementation.

STRATEGY AND DIVERSIFICATION

Present competitive conditions coupled with the restructuring of several major industries has forced firms to reassess their current product-market position. In some instances, firms have been pushed toward a strategy of diversification. This is typically the case with single-business or dominant-business firms that find themselves at the mature stage of an industry life cycle (see Figure 4.1), an often-used construct for explaining the pattern of product or industry growth.

Figure 4.1   Industry/Product Life Cycle

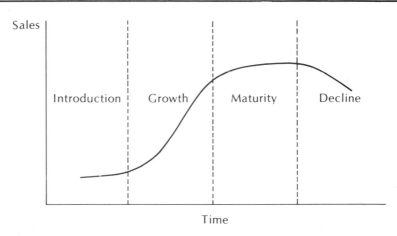

As Porter (1980) states:

> The hypothesis is that an industry passes through a number of phases or stages—introduction, growth, maturity, and decline. These stages are defined by inflection points in the rate of growth of industry sales. Industry growth follows an S-shaped curve because of the process of innovation and diffusion of a new product. The flat introductory phase of industry growth reflects the difficulty of overcoming buyer inertia and stimulating trials of the new product. Rapid growth occurs as many buyers rush into the market once the product has proven itself successful. Penetration of the product's potential buyers is eventually reached, causing the rapid growth to stop and level off to the underlying rate of growth of the relevant buyer group. Finally, growth will eventually taper off as new substitute products appear. (p. 157)

As Porter discusses, the life cycle construct has its limitations. For example, stages typically vary widely in duration from situation to situation. Also, in some instances stages may be skipped, and the S-shaped curve is not always observed. Nonetheless, this pattern seems to emerge across a number of settings and is a helpful tool for aiding strategic decision making.

For a single-business or dominant-business firm in the mature phase, the primary concern is for sources of future growth. (The problem is the same for a diversified firm if most of its businesses are mature.) To be sure, a number of such firms have attempted to invigorate their existing business through the introduction of new products and the use of new technologies directed at both the design of the product and the production process, as has been the case with U.S. automobile firms over the past five years.

Alternatively, a number of such firms have chosen to diversify away from the core business, thus lessening reliance upon it. For example, U.S. Steel is currently positioned in oil and gas, chemicals, resource development, fabricating and engineering, manufacturing, and transportation in addition to steel. American Can has diversified into consumer products, retailing, and financial services. Also, Esmark, once positioned only in meat packing (as Swift and Company) diversified into businesses in personal products and apparel, foods, industrial and agricultural chemicals, electronics, and industrial products, prior to their acquisition by Beatrice Foods.

Understanding how such strategic shifts occur and, more importantly, developing a framework that helps us to project a pattern of diversification leading to strong financial performance is a prime challenge. Some recent works hold considerable potential for advancing our understanding of how different patterns of strategic change require different organizational structures, management systems, and company cultures, and of how effective performance is attained.

ASSESSING RELATEDNESS

As stated earlier, and as some of the examples in the previous section indicate, a range of diversification strategies—from highly related to highly unrelated—can be observed. In order to understand the strategic choices available to firms and to be able to make meaningful prescriptive statements, a mechanism for operationalizing and assessing relatedness is critical.

Existing diversification studies are primarily focused on assessing the degree of diversification attained, toward which numerous approaches have been employed. Pitts and Hopkins (1982) have conducted an extensive literature review and summary on this topic. As they suggest, "the first tasks facing a researcher wishing to measure a firm's diversity therefore, is to identify its individual businesses" (p. 620). In this review of strategic diversity and its modes of operationalization, Pitts and Hopkins cite three primary approaches. The first, resource independence, sees a business as discrete from others of the corporation if the "resources involved are separate from those supporting the firm's other activities" (p. 621). The least-employed approach, due to data collection difficulties, defines businesses in terms of market discreteness. Finally, businesses can be defined in terms of product differences, viewing each product offering as a separate business. The latter approach is the basis of the often-employed Standard Industrial Classification system.

Accordingly, having identified a firm's business by one of these methods, one is then in a position to assess the firm's overall level of diversity. Pitts and Hopkins here note two primary approaches to the measurement of diversity. The first is based upon the *number* of businesses in which the firm is positioned as measured by either an absolute count, some ratio that accounts for relative size of business, or other related indices. The second approach is termed *strategic* and assesses diversity by either the relatedness of various businesses or the firm's historical growth pattern.

The most commonly utilized operationalization of firm diversity is the relatedness measure employed by Wrigley and Rumelt. As discussed earlier, Rumelt developed, as a variation of Wrigley's (1970) scheme, a typology that placed firms into four primary categories—single business, dominant business, related business, and unrelated business (all but single business having subcategories within)—according to the degree of strategic interdependence across businesses as well as "the proportion of a firm's revenues that can be attributed to its largest single business in a given year" (p. 14). Nathanson (1980) has developed a system that captures both product and market diversity.

Although such categorization schemes can effectively depict the firm's achieved strategy, assuming the availability of adequate and precise information allowing for the accurate categorization of each firm under study, it does so based upon aggregate business-level assessments that provide little detail at a more operational or functional level. Our contention is that while these schemes are somewhat effective in assessing relatedness across businesses in which the firm is already positioned, they provide little insight to the firm that is contemplating a specific diversification. That is, the schemes are not implementation oriented.

Viewing the organization in a more operational sense can lead to a germane view of relatedness. Focusing on the issue of diversification, several authors have argued that the firm is composed of resources beyond managerial or financial ones. Penrose (1959) stated that "the firm is essentially a pool of resources the utilization of which is organized in an administrative framework," and that "the final products being produced by a firm at any given time merely represents one of several ways in which the firm could be using its resources" (p. 150). Extending this logic, Teece (1980) has suggested that diversification is built upon the application of know-how from one domain to another, given the appropriate configuration of market and competitive conditions. Consistent with these views, Wernerfelt (1984) has proposed the utilization of corporate strategy matrices that track firm-specific skills against existing and potential market positions. This approach is a contrast to the commonly used Boston Consulting Group matrix, which categorizes the businesses of a firm according to industry attractiveness (rate of market growth) and the firm's competitive position (market share), which can lead to strategic choices being predicted primarily on financial data. (See Hofer and Schendel [1978] for a detailed discussion of portfolio theory and corporate-level strategy.) Finally, Burgelman (1984) suggests specific questions to help firms assess "operational relatedness." In the tradition of these more implementation-oriented perspectives of relatedness, we propose an alternative framework for conceptualizing relatedness and diversity.

AN ALTERNATIVE FRAMEWORK FOR CONCEPTUALIZING STRATEGIC DIVERSITY[1]

Although the literature reviewed in earlier chapters has extensively covered the research on the major strategic repositioning patterns pursued by industrial enterprise to date—vertical integration and product-market diversification—there are emerging strategies yet to be addressed. For example, some commodity firms such as chemical companies are shifting emphasis from their upstream commodity businesses to their downstream specialty chemical businesses. This major strategic change, accompanied by much organizational turmoil, is neither vertical integration nor diversification. Something more is happening, as suggested by changes at Monsanto (Smith 1983). The role of organizational and managerial variables in the success of such changes is no less critical than in other strategy implementation contexts. However, the conceptual constructs by which these issues will be framed are currently unfolding.

In examining the situation of vertically integrated companies, one can observe a variety of management practices. In contrast, there is a general lack of attention to the differences between upstream- or downstream-positioned firms. As an initial step in the assessment of this issue, the concept of center of gravity has been developed. This framework is useful to firms that are neither vertically integrating further nor diversifying but are nonetheless implementing a strategic shift.

---

1. The material in the remainder of this chapter is adapted from J. R. Galbraith, "Strategy and Organization Planning," *Human Resource Management* 22 (1/2) (Spring/Summer 1983): 63–77.

The center of gravity is a marriage and extension of the concepts of "driving force" (Tregoe and Zimmerman 1980) and "nexus" (Nathanson and Cassano 1982), and the value-added industry supply chain. The driving force idea is that each company has or should have a driving force, such as market served, products offered, or process technology. These forces correspond to many of the differences in the practices of the vertically integrated paper companies and also sometimes correspond with the stages of the industry supply chain.

A company establishes its center of gravity by starting operations in a particular industry at a particular stage of that industry. If and when it is successful, the company learns the management lessons of that stage of that industry. This point is important, because each stage of any industry has different success factors. Thus, the organization and its management are shaped by the lessons learned at their stage in an industry. Their values, their management systems, their business lessons, their organization, their path of succession, and their mind-sets are all shaped by the stage of initial success. They have established an anchor, or center of gravity. Strategic changes then take place through moves around and from this center of gravity.

To further explain the concept of center of gravity and its associated management implications, the example of the paper industry is employed. Figure 4.2 represents a modified value-added supply chain. It depicts not only the supply pattern and flow but also the distance from the ultimate consumer. Each industry has its stages; some have more or fewer stages. Service industries typically have fewer stages.

The chain begins with a raw material extraction stage, which supplies crude oil, iron ore, logs, or bauxite to the second stage of primary manufacturing. This second stage is a variety-reducing stage to produce a standardized output (petrochemicals, steel, paper pulp, or aluminum ingots). The next stage fabricates commodity

Figure 4.2   Supply Stages in a Manufacturing Industry

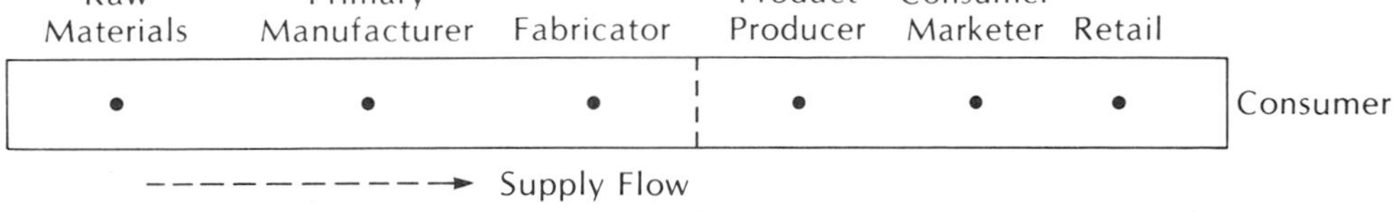

products from this primary material. Fabricators produce polyethylene, cans, sheet steel, cardboard cartons, and semiconductor components. The next stage is the product producers, who add value usually through product development, patents, and proprietary product features. The next stage is the manufacturer and marketer of consumer products. Next come the distributors and finally, the retailers, who sell to the final consumer. These companies add value by creating time and place utility.

The line splitting the chain into two segments divides the industry into upstream and downstream halves. While differences exist between each of the stages, the differences between the upstream and downstream stages are striking. The upstream stages add value by reducing the variety of raw materials found on the earth's surface to a few standard commodities. The purpose is to produce flexible, predictable raw materials and intermediate products from which an increasing variety of downstream products are made. The downstream stages add value through producing a variety of products to meet varying customer needs. The downstream value is added through advertising, product positioning, marketing channels, and R&D. Thus, the upstream and downstream companies face very different business problems and tasks.

Note that these distinctions are not universal. For example, some upstream companies, such as specialty chemical and steel firms, offer products differentiated from those of competitors in the broad market and are clearly not commodity producers. Other examples can be identified as well. However, for the majority of firms competing in the broad market (as opposed to niche positions), these contrasts are proposed as valid and meaningful. Further, other contrasts and characteristics across this dichotomy have implications for managerial choices and practices.

The reason for distinguishing between upstream and downstream companies is that the factors for success, the lessons learned by managers, and the organizations used are fundamentally different. The successful, experienced manager has been shaped and formed in fundamentally different ways in the different stages. The management processes are different, as are the dominant functions. In short, the company's culture is shaped by where it began in the industry chain. Listed in Table 4.1 are some fundamental differences that illustrate the contrast.

The mind-set of upstream managers is geared toward standardization and efficiency. They are the producers of standardized commodity products. In contrast, downstream managers try to customize and tailor output to diverse customer needs. They segment markets and target individual users. The upstream company wants to standardize to maximize the number of end users and get volume

**Table 4.1   Contrasting Characteristics
of Upstream and Downstream Companies**

Upstream	Downstream
Commodity	Proprietary
Standardize	Customize
Maximize End Users	Target End Users
Low-Cost Producers	High Margins
Sales Push	Marketing Pull
Line-Driven Organization	Line/Staff
Process Innovation	Product Innovation
Capital Budget	R&D/Advertising Budget
Capital Intensive	People Intensive
Technological Know-How	Marketing Skills
Supply & Trading/Manufacturing & Engineering	Product Development/ Marketing

to lower costs. The downstream company wants to target particular sets of end users. Therefore, the upstreamers have a divergent view of the world based on their commodity. For example, the cover of the 1981 annual report of Intel (a fabricator of commodity semiconductors) is a listing of the ten thousand uses to which microprocessors have been put. The downstreamers have a convergent view of the world based on customer needs and will select whatever commodity will best serve that need. Because of this contrast in mindsets, the electronics industry sees an ever-present conflict between the upstream component types and the downstream systems types.

The basis of competition is different in the two stages. Commodities compete on price, since the products are the same. Therefore, it is essential that the successful upstreamer be the low-cost producer. Their organizations are the lean and mean ones with a minimum of overheads. Low cost is also important for the downstreamer, but proprietary features generate high margins. That feature may be a brand image, such as Maxwell House, a patented technology, an endorsement (such as the American Dental Association's endorsement of Crest toothpaste), customer service policy, and so on. Competition centers on product features and product positioning more than on price. This means that marketing and product management set prices. Products move by marketing pull. In contrast, the upstream company pushes the product through a strong sales force. Salespeople often negotiate prices within limits set by top management.

The organizations are different as well. The upstream companies are functional and line-driven. They seek a minimum of staff, and even those staffs that are used are clearly in supporting roles. The downstream company with mutiple products and multiple markets learns to manage diversity early. Profit centers emerge, and resources need to be allocated across products and markets. Larger staffs arise to assist top management in priority setting across competing product-market areas. Higher margins permit the overhead to exist.

Both upstream and downstream companies use research and development. However, the upstream company invests in process development to lower costs. The downstream company invests primarily in product development to achieve proprietary positions.

The key managerial processes also vary. The upstream companies are driven by the capital budget and have various capital appropriations controls. The downstream companies also have a capital budget but are driven by the R&D budget (product producers) or the advertising budget (consumer products). Further downstream, working capital becomes paramount. Managers learn to control the business by managing the turnover of inventory and accounts receivable. Thus, the upstream company is capital intensive, and technological know-how is critical. Downstream companies are more people intensive. Therefore, the critical skills center on human resource management and marketing.

The dominant functions also vary with stages. The raw material processor is dominated by geologists, petroleum engineers, and traders. The supply and distribution function that searches for the most economical end use is powerful. The manufacturers of commodities are dominated by engineers who come up through manufacturing. The downstream companies are dominated by technologists in research and product development. Farther downstream, marketing and then merchandising emerge as the power centers. The line of succession to the CEO usually runs through this dominant function.

In summary, the upstream and downstream companies are very different entities. The differences, a bit exaggerated here because of the dichotomy, lead to differences in organizational structure, management processes, dominant functions, succession paths, and management beliefs and values—in short, the management way of life. Thus, companies can be in the same industry but be very different because they developed from a beginning at a particular stage of the industry. This beginning, and the initial successes, teach management the lessons of that stage. The firm develops an integrated organization (structure, processes, rewards, and people) that is peculiar to that stage and which forms the center of gravity.

STRATEGIC CHANGES

The concept of center of gravity allows us to talk about strategic changes in some different ways. The basic thrust of the argument is that strategic changes that do not involve changes to the center of gravity (such as vertical integration or related diversification) are easier to implement and historically have been more successful. Changes such as unrelated diversification and moves upstream or downstream require changes in the center of gravity and are much more difficult to implement successfully. The next section discusses major strategic changes. These include vertical integration; by-product, related, intermediate, and unrelated diversifications; and finally, a shift in center of gravity.

Vertical Integration

The first strategic change that an organization sometimes makes is to vertically integrate within its industry. At a certain size, the organization can move backward to prior stages to guarantee sources of supply and secure bargaining leverage on vendors. Alternatively (or in addition to the backward movement), it can move forward to guarantee markets and volume for capital investments, and become its own customer to feed back data for new products. This initial strategic move does not change the center of gravity, because the prior and subsequent stages are usually operated for the benefit of the center of gravity stage.

The paper industry is used to illustrate the concepts of center of gravity and vertical integration. Figure 4.3 depicts five paper companies that operate from different centers of gravity. The crosshatch indicates the extent of vertical integration and which stage is the center of gravity.

The first company is Weyerhaeuser. Its center of gravity is at the land and timber stage of the industry. Weyerhaeuser seeks the highest return use for a log. It makes pulp, paper rolls, containers, and milk cartons, but it is a timber company. If the returns are better in lumber, the pulp mills are fed with sawdust and chips. International Paper (the name of the company tells it all), by contrast, is a primary manufacturer of paper. It also has timberlands and container plants, and works on new products for aseptic packaging. However, if the pulp mills ran out of logs, the manager of the woodlands used to be fired. The raw material stage is to supply the manufacturing stage, not seek the highest return for its timber. The Container Corporation (again, the name describes the company) is an example of a

*Figure 4.3   Five Paper Companies
Operating at Different Centers of Gravity*

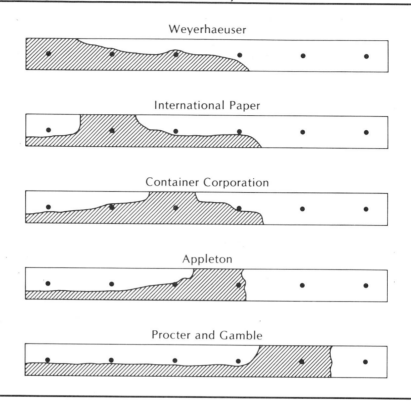

fabricator. It also has woodlands and pulp mills, but they are to supply the container-making operations. Appleton, which makes specialty paper products, is a product producer. For example, Appleton produces a paper with globules of ink embedded in it. When struck with an impact printer, the globules burst and form a letter or number.

The last company is Procter and Gamble, which is a consumer products company. Like the other companies, it also operates pulp mills and owns timberlands. The woodlands, however, is not a stand-alone profit center as it is at Weyerhaeuser. The woodlands is a function whose task is to supply the pulp mills, not make the highest return on a log. The business is driven by the advertising or marketing function. If one wanted to be CEO of Procter and Gamble, one would not run a pulp mill or the woodlands. The path to CEO is reached by becoming a brand manager for Charmin or Pampers.

Thus, each of the companies in Figure 4.3 is in the paper industry. Each operates at a number of stages in the industry, but each company is very different because it has its center of gravity at a different stage. The management system is also different at each company. The advertising budget is key at Procter and Gamble while the capital budget is key at International Paper. Other factors listed in Table 4.1 also vary.

Diversification

The next strategic change that a company usually takes is diversification. (A major move to an international market may take place at any time and is not discussed here.) The growth opportunities usually fade from the initial industry of birth, and opportunities are sought in other industries. As mentioned earlier, there are different types of diversification. They will be discussed here in order of increasing amount of strategic change required, difficulty in making the change, amount of diversity being adopted, and amount of decentralization in the organization that is needed to implement the strategy.

By-Product Diversification.   One of the first diversification moves that a vertically integrated company makes is to sell by-products from points along the industry chain. Figure 4.4 depicts this strategy. If one attributes revenue to the various industries in which the company operates, this company appears to be diversified. But the company has changed neither its industry nor its center of gravity. The company is behaving intelligently by seeking additional sources of revenue and profit. However, it is still psychologically committed to its center of gravity and to its industry. ALCOA is such a firm. Even though it operates several industries, its output varies directly with the aluminum cycle. It has not reduced its dependence on a single industry as one would with real diversification.

Figure 4.4   By-Product Diversification at ALCOA

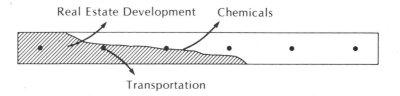

A key dimension that distinguishes among companies pursuing this strategy is the number of industries into which by-products are sold. As discussed earlier in this chapter, although the simple number of industries is an imperfect measure of overall diversity, in this case it may well be the most salient. The higher the number of industries to which by-products are sold, the greater the decentralization required. However, the need for decentralization here is not as great as is needed with subsequent diversification strategies.

Related Diversification.   Related diversification is a strategic change in which the company moves from its core industry into other industries that are related to the core industry. As mentioned earlier, researchers are trying to define relatedness and to distinguish degrees of relatedness between industries. The position taken here is that relatedness has two dimensions. One is the degree to which the new industry is related to the core industry. The other is the degree to which the company operates at the same center of gravity in the new industry. The latter is the more important. The proposition here is that related diversification can occur only when a company enters a related industry at the same center of gravity. An example will best illustrate this.

Procter and Gamble is a good example of a related diversifier. Beginning with the manufacture of soaps, it rounded out its line with body soaps, luxury soaps, and cleansers. It then moved into shortening (Crisco) and cooking oils, which were made from some of the same ingredients, using similar process technologies, and which were based on similar chemical technologies. A next step was adding shortening to flour to create prepared mixes for cakes, biscuits, and so on. At this point, Proctor and Gamble purchased the Duncan Hines trademark. Another effort was aimed at the dentifrice market. Again, this effort played off similar technologies already in-house. Their effort successfully culminated in the introduction of Crest toothpaste.

All of these strategic moves diversified the Procter and Gamble portfolio. The company reduced its dependence on some cyclical raw material commodities such as tallow oil. However, each business was very similar to soap. The product and process technologies were similar, a single central purchasing organization bought all materials, all products were packaged on lines, all were delivered by trucks and distributed through grocery wholesalers and chains, and all were sold by a single sales force. But most important, each strategic move resulted in a branded product, sold primarily by advertising to the homemaker and managed by a brand manager.

More recent strategic moves by Procter and Gamble have entered it into the paper, pharmaceuticals, coffee, and beverage industries.

Each of these moves involves learning different process and product technologies, manufacturing skills, and forced integration—backward into purchasing forests and forward into soft drink bottling. The recent changes are clearly less related to the soap business. As a result, Procter and Gamble has entered these businesses by acquisition to acquire not only the assets but also the expertise. However, each of these businesses is also a branded consumer product (Folger's, Orange Crush, Pampers, Charmin, and so on), which is distributed mostly through grocery wholesalers and chains, and is sold to the homemaker. Each business is run by advertising and managed by a brand manager. In short, each business has the same center of gravity.

Figure 4.5 is a schematic attempt to depict the points just described. It shows Procter and Gamble in a number of different businesses. The figure indicates that Procter and Gamble has pursued different levels of integration in each business. Also, the farther from the soap business, the less related are the industries into which Procter and Gamble has diversified. Soap is closer to shortening than to soft drinks and is closer to a dentifrice than to paper. However, every single business is run as a consumer-branded product business. Each is run by brand managers in advertising. The center of gravity is the same in each business. Procter and Gamble has entered a variety of industries but always at the same center of gravity. It must learn a new industry and a new business in that industry with each strategic change. However, it does not have to learn a new way of doing business.

Thus, related diversification is a strategic change in which the company diversifies by entering new industries but always enters business in that industry at the same center of gravity. Variation sitll remains in the amount of relatedness. For example, Procter and Gamble and General Mills are both companies that operate at the consumer-branded products center of gravity by selling to the homemaker through a brand or product management system. But General Mills is less related because it has gone into toys and games, fashion merchandise, and restaurants (Red Lobster). A scale of relatedness could perhaps be constructed by listing the functional aspects of any business, such as those shown in Table 4.2, and deciding whether that aspect is related or unrelated. A scale of 0 to 19 could be constructed to get an estimate of relatedness.

An appreciation for the degree of relatedness is needed to estimate the amount of strategic change that is being attempted. The less related the diversification, the greater the difficulty of strategy implementation, and the greater the likelihood of acquisition versus internal growth. The greater will be the political problems that will have to be managed, and the more decentralized will be the organi-

Figure 4.5 Procter and Gamble Diversified

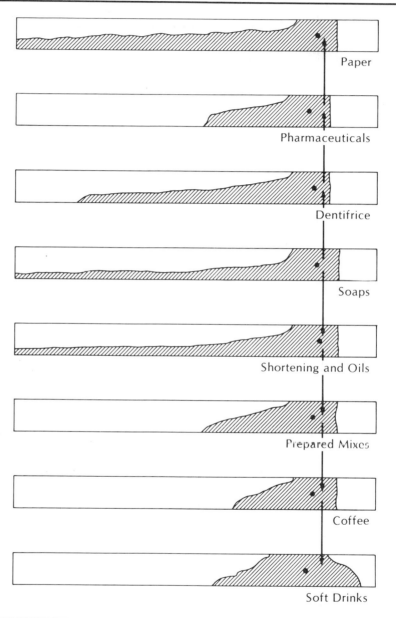

Paper

Pharmaceuticals

Dentifrice

Soaps

Shortening and Oils

Prepared Mixes

Coffee

Soft Drinks

Table 4.2 Business Functional Aspects

	Related	Unrelated
1. Process Technology		
2. Product Technology		
3. Product Development		
4. Purchasing		
5. Assembly		
6. Packaging		
7. Shipping		
8. Inventory Management		
9. Quality		
10. Labor Relations		
11. Distribution		
12. Selling		
13. Promotion		
14. Advertising		
15. Consumer/Customer		
16. Buying Habits		
17. Capital (Fixed)		
18. Working Capital		
19. Credit		

zational structure. The magnitude of the strategy implementation problem is directly proportional to the amount of relatedness in the diversification move. The number of industries into which a company diversifies is also an indicator of diversity, but here, that indicator is less important.

The same argument can be made at different centers of gravity. Dayton-Hudson is a related diversifier in retailing (Dayton's, Target, B. Dalton Booksellers, Mervyns, and so on), as is Sears Roebuck. Clearly, Sears' move into financial services makes it less related but still focused at retail levels. Dayton-Hudson grows through internal start-ups. Sears has recently relied on acquisition. Dow-Corning bases its businesses on developing new products from silicon chemistry and driving its strategy through R&D. 3M does the same, but it is more diverse. However, 95 percent of 3M's revenue comes from products based on coating and bonding technologies. Both companies operate at a center of gravity around product development using a common product technology.

Intermediate Diversification. Between related and unrelated diversifiers are a large number of firms whose businesses are somewhat related but operate at a number of—usually a few—centers of gravity. This strategic change is hypothesized to be more difficult because it involves managing businesses with different centers of gravity. In some respects, it is similar to Rumelt's category of related-linked diversifiers (Rumelt 1974). This type of change has two dimensions. The first dimension is simply the number of centers of gravity at which the company's businesses operate. The second dimension is the distance between the centers. Clearly, the greater the number of centers and the greater the distances between them, the greater the amount of strategic change. Some examples will illustrate this point.

An organization that has engaged in a minimal amount of intermediate diversification is Motorola. The company is depicted in Figure 4.6. Motorola started as a producer of mobile communications equipment (car radios, walkie-talkies, mobile phones, pagers, and so on). It has added other communications products to fill out its line. Motorola next diversified by setting up a separate unit to work with the military when the volume was sufficient. The company then made a major thrust in semiconductors as its own needs became significant.

Figure 4.6 Diversification at Motorola

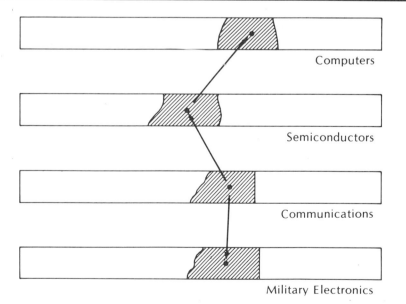

Computers

Semiconductors

Communications

Military Electronics

The semiconductor business was very successful and began to supply all companies, including competitors of its sister divisions. The move was not operated as a vertical integration but more as a diversification. The semiconductor business operates as a fabricator of commodity memory chips, power transitors, logic circuits, and so on. As such, it has a different center of gravity than does the communications business. It is also managed as a separate business. Motorola's corporate headquarters has much less influence over the business than does Procter and Gamble's corporate office over its businesses. The power center at Motorola is the group or sector level at semiconductors and communications. Subsequently, Motorola entered the computer business via acquisition, but it does not operate semiconductors and computers as vertically integrated units.

Motorola thus operates with a low amount of intermediate diversification. Because it has entered a number of businesses, the company is diverse. These businesses have some relatedness because they are all electronics based. However, unlike Procter and Gamble, Morotola operates the two main parts of the company at different centers of gravity. The centers are, however, adjacent in the supply chain. The management systems are different, but minimally so.

An organization that is becoming more of an intermediate diversifier is Union-Camp. The strategic changes are shown in Figure 4.7. Union-Camp is a top performer among the primary manufacturing companies in the pulp and paper industry. Like other paper companies, it vertically integrated into forest operations. Union-Camp also began to enter the plywood, lumber, and fiberboard businesses, and began selling chemicals as by-products of the pulp- and papermaking processes. All of these are manufacturing businesses that make commodity products. More recently, Union-Camp acquired a retail lumber business and a specialty chemicals business. These acquisitions are operated as separate subsidiaries, not as vertically integrated units.

Union-Camp has embarked on a difficult strategic change. Even though it operates in fewer industries than do Procter and Gamble and Motorola, it operates at three different centers of gravity. In addition, these three centers are spread across the supply chain in upstream and downstream positions. Union-Camp has to learn to manage three markedly different ways of doing business. The organization will be a mixed model.

Other examples can be given, but the point is that operating at different centers of gravity poses significant management problems. In addition, if these centers are spread between retailing and primary manufacturing, the strategic change is even more difficult. Nathanson's findings support these assertions (Nathanson 1980). Using a concept similar to center of gravity, he found that the greater

Figure 4.7 Strategic Moves at Union-Camp

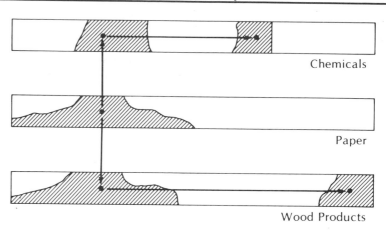

Chemicals

Paper

Wood Products

the number of centers at which a company operated, the lower was its economic performance. He did not include, however, any measure of distance between centers.

The discussion so far has introduced four different dimensions of diversity. The first was the number of different industries in which a company operates. This measure of diversity is the simplest and will distinguish among by-product diversifiers. But the strategic implementation problems occur when the new industries are different from those in which the company already operates. The second measure of relatedness assumed that the company operated at the same center of gravity but entered businesses where other business functions were different, such as process technology, customer buying behavior, and so on. The third measure was the number of different centers of gravity at which a company operates. This measure, up to a point, indicates a greater amount of strategic change. The company must learn not only new businesses but also new ways of doing business. The fourth measure is the distances between the centers; that is, differences between ways of doing business is proportional to the distance on the industry supply chain.

Unrelated Diversification. The last category is an extension of the prior discussion on diversity. The intermediate diversifiers operate at a few centers of gravity in a few industries with some relatedness (e.g., electronics, energy) between them. The unrelated have several centers of gravity, operate in many industries, and actually seek to avoid relatedness. They have no psychological commitment to any industry or group of related industries. They always change by acquisition and divestiture. Textron and Teledyne are still the paradigm examples.

The possibility exists to create a scale or scales for diversity by combining the dimensions described here. Such a scale would make empirical testing of large samples more feasible. Instead, this chapter has attempted to identify some clinical types. Implied was an ordinal scale of diversity. Such a scale and classification are needed to better understand the problems of strategy implementation.

The intermediate and unrelated diversifiers do not change the centers of gravity of their core business. They have to fashion a corporate headquarters to manage businesses operating at different centers of gravity. For example, American Can was in the packaging business, manufacturing metal, plastic, and paper packaging products. The company was run with a centralized divisional organization with about 1,500 people on the corporate staff. During the 1980s, American Can has been redeploying its assets by first selling the paper packaging component. It then made acquisitions in specialty retailing and financial services, and is looking for yet another business. To manage these new businesses plus the packaging businesses, a new corporate headquarters organization was created with a corporate staff of 300 people. The packaging business is still a major part of the company, but it still operates at its previous center of gravity. The new acquisitions have different centers of gravity that American Can must learn to manage, but they have not changed the center of gravity of the packaging business. The diversification at American Can then is different from the strategic changes where the company is not diversifying into new industries, but is shifting centers of gravity in its existing industry.

Changes in Center of Gravity

The research on strategic changes has centered largely on diversification. This result is surprising, since many of the strategic changes that organizations are trying to implement are not of this nature. The popular press describes DEC and Monsanto as trying to move downstream in their industry, while Johnson and Johnson and American Hospital Supply are trying to move upstream. The second reason for surprise is that changing the center of gravity is probably the most difficult strategic change to make. Why? Because it involves large-scale change in all of the organizational dimensions. A center of gravity shift requires a dismantling of the current power structure, rejection of parts of the old culture, and establishing all new management systems. Related diversification works for exactly the opposite reasons. The company can move into new businesses with minimal change to the power structure and accepted ways of doing things. Changes in the center of gravity usually occur by new start-ups at a new center of gravity rather than by a shift in the center of established firms.

At times during the 1970s, after nationalization by OPEC, and in the 1980s when oil "gluts" occurred, the oil companies all wanted to be downstream profitable. That is, during shortages and normal times with depletion allowances, the money was made at the well-head. The upstream companies were integrated, but the retail outlets were to get rid of the oil that was pumped. The new circumstances require that the downstream operations pay for themselves and make money. However, this change requires a power shift to marketing from the engineers, geologists, and supply and distribution people. In companies where top management comes from the latter functions, the change has not occurred. The companies that are successful are those that began as downstream companies and established their center of gravity there. Amerada Hess is an example. Leon Hess himself started in the business by driving delivery trucks. He knows the retail-distribution side of the business. The upstream companies have had great difficulty. Some have sold their downstream operations and have tried to diversify into unrelated areas. Others have defined themselves as raw material and energy companies, and have diversified into coal, uranium, and other mining and extractive industries. These diversifiers are having their problems in running multiple businesses. But the latter will require no change in the center of gravity. They should be the better performers over the long run.

Some exceptions prove the rule. For example, some organizations have shifted from upstream commodity producers to downstream product producers and consumer products firms. General Mills moved from a flour miller to a related diversified provider of products for the homemaker. Over a long period of time, the company shifted downstream into consumer food products from its Gold Medal flour cake mix product beginnings. From there, they diversified into related areas after selling off most of the milling operations—the old core of the company. NL Industries is another example. Originally the National Lead Corporation (now NL Industries), the company used an intermediate diversification strategy to get into oil drilling services. When demand for lead dropped, NL moved into lead-based paints and from there into various drilling muds. During the 1970s, NL used this entry point to expand the services provided to the drilling industry. They also sold off the old lead business. In both cases, however, new management was brought in, and acquisition and divestment were used to make the transition. Even though vestiges of the old name remain, these companies are substantially different.

STRATEGY AND STRUCTURE

Given this new view of strategy and diversification, it is appropriate to review their relationship to organizational structure. The relationships discussed are summarized in Table 4.3.

One can still find organizations staying in their original business. Such a single business is Wrigley, the chewing gum manufacturer. These organizations have a centralized functional structure. The next strategic type is the vertically integrated by-product seller. Again, these companies have some diversification but remain committed to their industry and center of gravity. The companies are also functional, but the sequential stages are often operated as profit center divisions. The companies are usually quite centralized and run by collegial management groups. The profit centers are not true ones in that they do not independently run their own businesses. These companies are almost all upstream.

The related businesses are those that move into new industries at their center of gravity. These companies are usually downstream. They adopt the decentralized profit center divisions; however, the divisions are not completely decentralized. These companies usually have strong corporate staffs and some centralized marketing, manufacturing, and R&D. The corporate payroll may have several thousand people on it.

The clearest contrast to the related diversifier is the unrelated business company. These companies enter a variety of businesses at several centers of gravity. The organization they adopt is the very

Table 4.3   Strategies and Associated Structures

Strategy	Structure
Single business	Functional
Vertical by-products	Functional with profit centers
Related businesses	Divisional
Intermediate businesses	Mixed structures
Unrelated businesses	Holding company

decentralized holding company. Their outstanding feature is the small corporate staff. Depending on the companies' size, the staff numbers range between fifty and two hundred, and they are usually support staffs. All of the marketing, manufacturing, and R&D is decentralized to the divisions. Group executives have no staffs and are generally corporate oriented.

The intermediate companies are neither of these extremes. Their forms are often transitory. The organizations that they utilize are usually mixed forms that are not easily classified. Some divisions are autonomous, while others are managed out of the corporate headquarters. Still others have strong group executives with group staffs. Some work has been done on classifying these structures (Allen 1978). Virtually no work has been done on center of gravity changes and their changes in structure.

SUMMARY AND MANAGERIAL IMPLICATIONS

The vast majority of research to date has examined selected changes in strategic positioning, primarily vertical integration and product-market diversification. Issues related to the shift in strategic emphasis and importance that the firm places across existing businesses, and the associated implications for strategy implementation, remain largely unexplained.

A central concept to understanding and proposing diversification strategies is relatedness. Typically, three prime modes have been used to define what constitutes an individual business: (1) resource separateness, (2) market discreteness, and (3) product differences. The modes must then be matched with an overall assessment of diversity. Such assessments are either numerical, including various counting, ratio, and indexing schemes, or based upon relatedness categories, such as those employed by Wrigley, Rumelt, and Nathanson.

An alternative framework, more implementation oriented in character, is proposed. Building upon the various stages of the vertical integration chain, each firm can be said to have a center of gravity that arises from the firm's position of success, strength, and dominant operations. Further, the characteristics of what are termed upstream and downstream companies are vastly different. Relatedness is viewed in a more operational, functional manner within this framework.

Given this view, a broader range of strategic options is open to the firm, including by-products diversification, related diversification, intermediate diversification, unrelated diversification, and center of gravity change. Each strategy has an associated organizational structure, consistent with the discussions in Chapters 2 and 3. Based on the preceding, several managerial implications are worth noting:

1. A firm's center of gravity has a strong influence on diversification options and success.

    a. *Firms need a center of gravity.* One major issue for firms that are vertically integrated to some extent is whether there should be a center of gravity. Our view is that there should be one. If not, management attention will go into transfer price and supply disputes along the vertically integrated chain. The center of gravity provides strategic focus and order. For example, at Procter and Gamble the manager of the woodlands operations knows his or her role. Political power struggles are minimized, allowing attention to be focused on eternal competitiors. As to whether the firm can have more than one center of gravity, the answer depends upon how the firm is managed. If separated and run as separate subsidiaries, the answer is yes. However, if the firm attempts to run equally dominant stages in an integrated fashion, difficulties will emerge. Clearly, additional research is in order in this area.

    b. *Upstream companies are poor diversifiers.* Research findings indicate that the poorest performer of the strategic categories is the vertically integrated by-product seller (Rumelt 1974). These companies are all upstream, raw material, and primary manufacturers. They make up a good portion of "Smokestack America." In some respects, these companies made their money early in the century, and their value-added is shifting to lesser-developed countries in the natural course of industrial development. However, significant here is their inability to change. No secret to anyone is that these companies have been underperformers, yet they have continued to put money back into the same business.

    Our explanation focuses on the center of gravity. These previously successful companies put together an organization that fit their industry and stage. When the industry declined, they were unable to change as well as the downstream companies. The reason is that upstream companies were functional organizations with few general managers. Their resource allocation was within a single business, not across multiple products. The management skills are partly technological know-how. This technology does not transfer across industries at the primary manufacturing center of gravity. The knowledge of papermaking does not help very much in glassmaking. Yet, both might be combined in a packaging company. Also, the capital intensity of these industries limits the diversification. Usually, one industry must be chosen and capital invested to be the low-cost producer. Thus, these companies have been notoriously poor diversifiers for a number of reasons.

   c. *Changing a firm's center of gravity offers particular challenges.* No mater where an organization is along the industry chain, changing centers of gravity is difficult. The reason is that a center of gravity shift requires a dismantling of the current power structure, rejection of parts of the old culture, and establishing all new management systems. Related diversification works for exactly the opposite reasons. These companies can move into new businesses with minimal change to the power structure and accepted ways of doing things. Changes in the center of gravity usually occur by new start-ups at a new center of gravity rather than by a shift in the center of established firms. Although successful cases can be cited (General Mills), the recent efforts and experiences of the companies make the point.

2. Center of gravity, in addition to the degree of diversification, is a prime determinant of organizational structure, systems, and processes. As discussed in this chapter, the upstream and downstream companies differ radically in terms of resource allocation processes, managerial skills, and priority tasks. Further, different functions dominate in one company versus the other. This idea is extended in subsequent chapters.

5

Processes and Systems for Managing Diversity

The phenomena that constitute organizations are not only structural in nature. There are also integrating processes, resource allocation processes, information systems, and many others, all of which constitute the form of organization. This chapter looks at organizational processes and systems used to cope with problems associated with various product-market strategies. A number of information-sharing and decision-making processes have been developed to integrate and coordinate activities, particularly those that cut across divisional and departmental boundaries. These processes vary from simple spontaneous meetings to complicated matrix forms. First we specify these processes and identify conditions under which different processes should be matched to different strategies and environmental conditions. We subsequently examine resource allocation processes and other information systems. The chapter concludes with a summary and statement of managerial implications.

INTEGRATING PROCESSES

All organizations must differentiate their structures so that each department or unit is assigned a task commensurate with the firm's strategy and environment. To an extent, each department, be it a function or a product division, can be seen to face a different subenvironment. The discussion of this choice of how to differentiate or structure the firm comprises much of Chapters 2 through 4.

Additionally, however, the firm must also integrate those differentiated functions around the interdependencies between them, as determined by the key competitive requirements of the strategy and industry. For those firms where new product introduction is the key competitive issue, the integration problem is one of coordinating marketing with research and development. Where on-time delivery to the customer is the key competitive issue, the integrating problem is one of coordinating marketing and production.

Therefore, the most effective firms are those that have differentiated their structures to the extent needed to adapt to various subenvironments and that simultaneously use mechanisms to integrate those differentiated structures to deal with the competitive issues of the overall corporate environment (Lawrence and Lorsch 1967).

Table 5.1 shows the different mechanisms that can be used to integrate departmental activities. Four of the mechanisms constitute standard practice in almost all instances. The hierarchy of authority is the principal mechanism used to resolve interdepartmental problems. The problem is referred upward to a common superior who oversees all departments affected by the problem. When a problem arises frequently, a rule or procedure is devised for it as a substitute for hierarchical referral. Other problems are best solved on the spot, so goals are set by way of planning processes such as scheduling and budgeting. Organizational control shifts from control over behavior to control over results, and discretion over actions to achieve results is decentralized. Exceptions to goals and rules are either referred to the hierarchy or are resolved on the spot through direct contact between affected parties. The informal, spontaneous processes serve as another substitute for hierarchical referral.

Studying the most effective firms in three industries, Lawrence and Lorsch (1967) found that some firms require more mechanisms for coordination. As Table 5.2 indicates, food processing firms and plastics firms need more than the standard practices. In contrast to

Table 5.1   Integrating Mechanisms

- Hierarchy
- Rules
- Goal Setting (Planning)
- Direct Contact
- Interdeparmental Liaison Roles
- Temporary Task Forces
- Permanent Teams
- Integrating Roles
- Integrating Departments

Table 5.2   Integrating Mechanisms Used in Three Different Industries

	Plastics	**Food**	**Container**
% New products in last 20 years	35%	15%	0%
Integrating devices	Rules	Rules	Rules
	Hierarchy	Hierarchy	Hierarchy
	Goal setting	Goal setting	Goal setting
	Direct contact	Direct contact	Direct contact
	Teams at 3 levels	Task forces	
	Integrating Dept.	Integrators	
%Integrators/ managers	22%	17%	0%

Source: Jay Galbraith, DESIGNING COMPLEX ORGANIZATIONS, © 1973, Addison-Wesley, Reading, Massachusetts. Pg. 111, Table II. Reprinted with permission.

the effective container firm, they have evolved cross-functional teams and task forces to manage the activity associated with the introduction of new products. These group mechanisms are actually substitutes for the general manager. The general manager would make these decisions under less variable and less diverse conditions. Also, new roles were created to help integrate the cross-departmental new product activities. Product managers were created to cope with diverse product lines and new product creation. These, too, are general manager equivalents. Pieces of general management work needed to coordinate interfunctional work when introducing new products are delegated to groups and integrating roles. But this delegation occurs only under conditions of diversity and uncertainty. The added managerial effort was not needed for the more predictable and less diverse container industry.

Overall, then, a number of specific mechanisms are used to achieve interdepartmental coordination. These mechanisms vary from hierarchial referral to the addition of integrating departments such as product management departments. Organizations select from the list those mechanisms that will permit them to implement their strategy. The selection is not random, however; choice makes a difference.

The list of coordination mechanisms as presented in Table 5.1 is an ordered list. Each step down the list represents the commitment to a more complicated and more expensive mechanism of coordination. The increasing expenditure of resources for coordination results, first, because integrating departments are more expensive than temporary task forces using line managers. But expenditures increase also, because mechanisms at the bottom of the list are added to, not substituted for, those high on the list. They are not direct substitutes. The plastics organization uses all coordination mechanisms. Therefore, an organization should select from the list starting at the top and going down only as far as is necessary to implement its strategy. The successful container firm stopped at direct contact, the successful food processor stopped with integrators (product managers), and the plastics firm adopted all of them to be successful. The costs of these mechanisms can be seen by examining the percentage of managers who play integrating, as opposed to line, roles. These figures are shown at the bottom of Table 5.2. In the plastics organization, 22 percent of the managers work in product management activities, yet they have a functional organization. In contrast, the container firm has no managers working in integrating roles. The difference is attributable to the amount of new product introduction that must be undertaken to remain competitive in the industry, and the level of technology required to support the new products. The more new product activity, and the higher the level of technology and uncertainty, the more the hierarchy needs to be buttressed with cross-departmental coordination mechanisms. Therefore, those organizations pursuing strategies characterized by interdepartmental activity, high uncertainty, and high diversity will select mechanisms farther down on the list than those organizations pursuing strategies characterized by low uncertainty and diversity.

Strategies characterized by high uncertainty and diversity require, at a minimum, the use of cross-departmental processes, usually in the form of teams, and integrating roles, usually in the form of program or product managers (Corey and Star 1971). If enough cross-functional program or product activity is ongoing, integrating departments may be created. For example, Figure 5.1 depicts product management departments (directorates) that are overlaid on a basic functional structure. This approach is a response to product diversification strategies designed when size limits the creation of multidivisional structures, sometimes in the presence of significant economies of scale in one or more functions as well. The observation has been made that organizations experience diversity in markets as well as in products, and so adopt market-based integrating departments. An example was IBM meeting the need to tailor the same product lines to government and commercial markets, and to distinguish between manufacturing, retailing, and banking submarket applications within commercial markets. Other organizations, such as Du Pont, have experienced both market and product diversity. The response of these organizations has been to organize simultaneously

***Figure 5.1 Monsanto Organic Chemicals Division Illustrating
Product Management Directorates and Functional Organization***

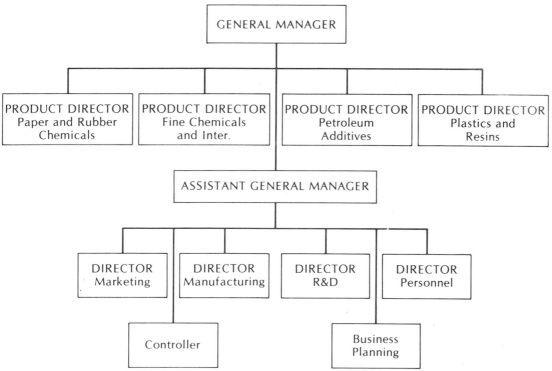

Source: E. Raymond Corey and Steven H. Star, *Organization Strategy: A Marketing Approach.* Boston: Division of Research, Harvard Business School, 1971, p. 346. Reprinted by permission.

by markets, products, and functions. A Du Pont Fibers organization is shown in Figure 5.2. The integrating departments are located in marketing to coordinate with the regional sales force and to take a marketing focus. The geographic sales force is concerned with the short-run approach to clients in their area. The industry market groups are concerned with intermediate-term issues such as market strategy, forecasts, promotions, and coordination with field sales. The product managers are concerned with longer-run issues of product strategy, new product development, product scheduling, and coordination with manufacturing and research. Thus, diversity is handled within functional organizations by developing integrating roles around the sources of diversity.

Figure 5.2   Du Pont Fibers Organization Showing
Industrial Market and Product Integrating Departments

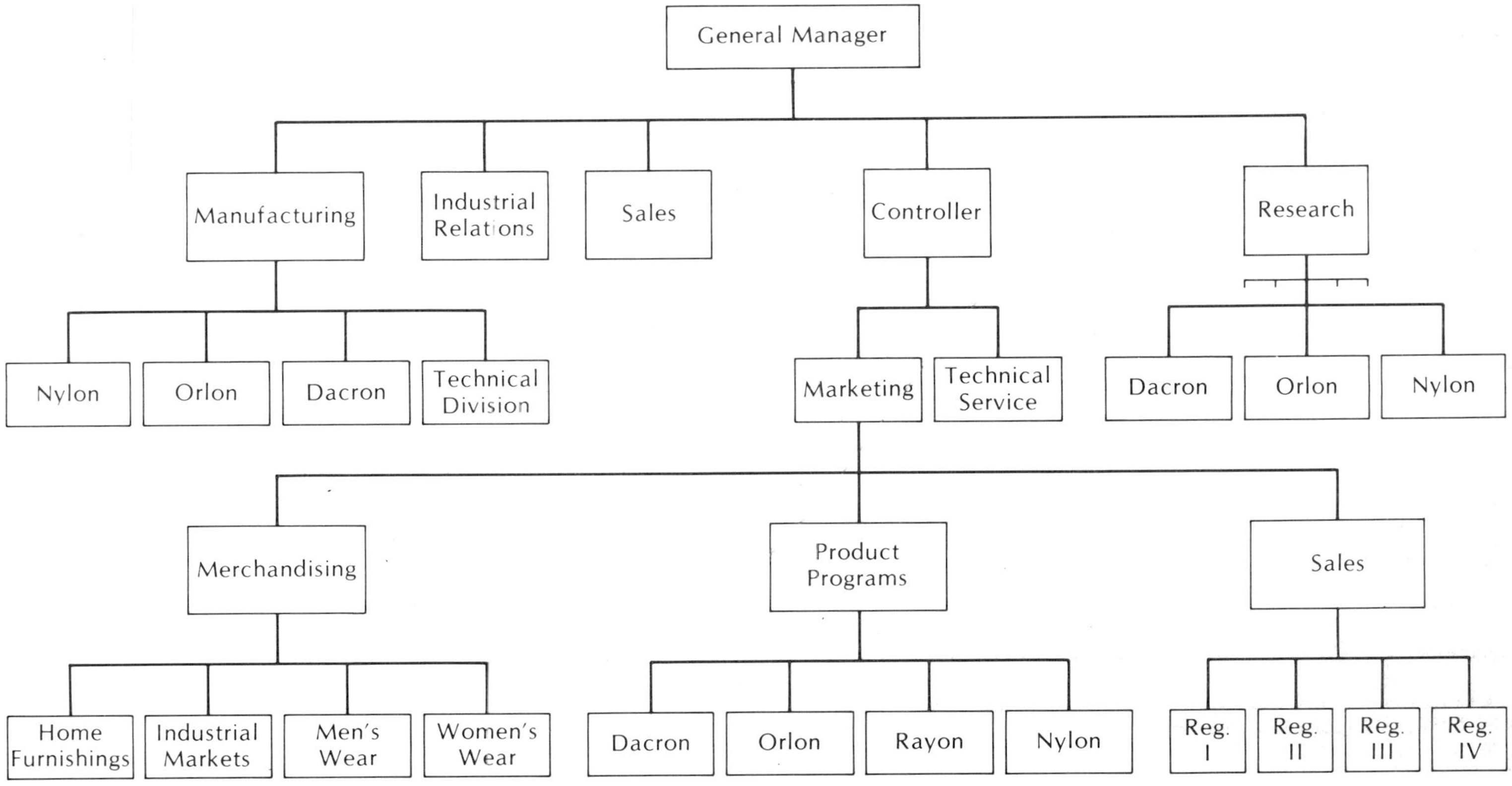

In their study of these issues, Corey and Starr noted that the greater the diversity and the greater the amount of new product introduction, the greater the likelihood of integrating roles and departments, and the greater was their influence. Thus, integrating roles represents one of the principal means with which to implement diversification strategies without reorganizing into a product divisionalized structure.

Simultaneous, or Matrix, Structures

The adoption of coordination mechanisms with which functional organizations can manage diversity suggests that a number of transition phases exist between the functional and multidivisional structures. Indeed, each step down the list of coordination mechanisms represents a step toward more product-oriented decision making. Thus, the change from functional to product structures need not be a major discrete alteration but can be an evolutionary movement. There is a continuous range of distribution of influence between product and functional orientations. This description is shown in Figure 5.3. One moves along the distribution of influence by adding additional coordination mechanisms and adding power to integrating roles. The point at which product and function are of equal power is called the matrix organization. At that point, there are simultaneously two line organizations of equal power. The organization is simultaneously functional and product. Equal power is obtained through multiple authority relations.

The chart for such a company is shown in Figure 5.4. It shows a matrix organization for a geographically organized bank that is pursuing a strategy of segmenting markets and creating new financial services for those markets. The resulting market diversity forces the bank into a simultaneous structure built around markets and geography. At some point, the two structures must intersect. In Figure 5.4 the market organization and geographic organization intersect at the country level. The individual who manages multinational corporate banking in a specific country has two bosses: the country manager and the market manager. The task of that individual is to integrate the two perspectives for that business in that country.

One could also move to the right-hand side of the diagram in Figure 5.3, where the product divisions are dominant and the functional managers play integrating roles. This form was the one adopted by the Commercial Airplane Division of Boeing as it diversified its product line. Thus, organizers are not faced with a choice of function versus product (or market or geography) divisions, but with a choice of whether to give priority to product or function.

Figure 5.3 **The Range of Alternatives**

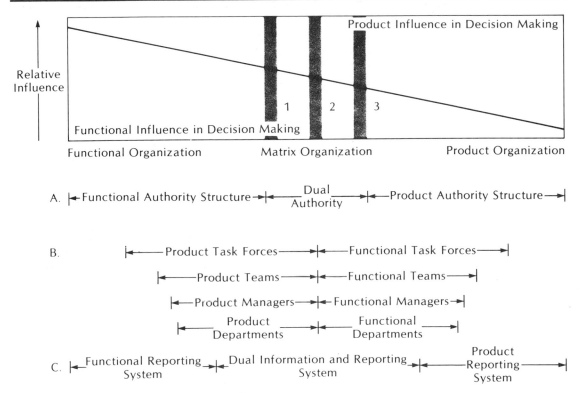

Organizations nowadays are simultaneous structures (simply a generalization of line staff models), with product and functional managers reporting to the general manager. Multinational firms add a third geographic dimension. Which dimension is more influential and has higher priority depends upon several factors, including the strategy and the business environment.

Several factors favor emphasizing the product side. As already mentioned, diversity and new product introductions are best managed through product-oriented structures. One would move to the right side of Figure 5.3 as a result. Also, increasing interdependence among functional departments and increased need for responsiveness to the market favor a product or project orientation. However, these generalizations must be qualified by considerations of size. Self-contained product divisions may be too small to have their own

Figure 5.4   Worldwide Matrix for a Banking Firm

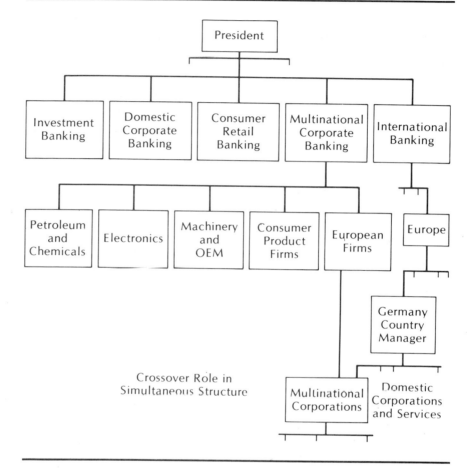

Crossover Role in
Simultaneous Structure

sales force or to achieve size economies in production. Therefore, the larger the organization, the more likely the establishment of product or project divisions. The smaller the organization, the more likely the establishment of product or project integrating departments. The longer the life cycle of the product or project the more likely that a self-contained division will be created.

Several factors favor the functional organization. Economies of scale in the functions mitigate against breaking them up and distributing the pieces among the product divisions. The need for special expertise and career paths for specialists is facilitated by the functional form. Therefore, firms pursuing state-of-the-art technology should have strong technical functions. The uncertainty connected with high technology also argues for a coordination capability across functions. The high-technology firms usually adopt some form of the matrix, which simultaneously gives them high technology and high coordination.

The general business environment also influences the organization's strategy. Galbraith (1973) describes how the business environment has shifted in the aerospace industry and how organizational structures have been adopted in order for the firms to remain competitive. These changes are independent of considerations based on size, product diversity, technology, and so on.

In the late 1950s and early 1960s, technical performance was the critical dimension. The environment was characterized by Sputnik, the space race, and the missile gap. The U.S. goverment deemed it imperative to produce technical accomplishments and to do so rapidly. The priorities placed technical performance first, schedule second, and cost a poor third. Data on actual performance during this period reflect this order of priorities. All projects met or exceeded technical specifications, but completion times were 1.5 times as great as projected, and costs exceeded targets by a factor of 3.2. In aerospace firms performing these projects, the functional managers dominated the joint decisions, but project managers were also influential because of time pressures. Since technical performance dominated other considerations, the influence distribution was approximated by the dotted line 1 in Figure 5.3.

In the early and middle 1960s, the environment changed. This period was called the McNamara era. Robert McNamara believed that technical performance could be achieved, but at less cost. The contracts changed from cost plus fixed fee to various incentive contracts and fixed price contracts. Defense Department officials demanded that aerospace firms use PERT, then PERT/Cost information systems. The effect of these changes was to make the project mananger more influential in the decision process. In Figure 5.3 the influence distribution was represented by the dotted line 2.

Still another change occurred in the late 1960s. Strong pressures to reduce defense costs began to operate. First was the publicity concerning cost overruns on the giant C-5A aircraft. Senator William Proxmire began hearings on contractor efficiency practices. Finally, inflation and shifting national priorities combined to make cost the top priority, as opposed to technical performance and schedule completion. In the internal workings of aerospace firms, the project managers began to dominate the joint decision processes. The pattern of influence was explicit. Project managers held vice-presidential status, whereas laboratory and functional managers had the title of director. The influence distribution moved to line 3 in Figure 5.3.

By the late 1970s, still another change was occurring. The national government shifted spending away from aerospace projects. The effect was to reduce the size of the aerospace industry and of firms in it. The firms had to retain specialized personnel to create the technology while meeting demands to reduce costs and size. Thus, the effective utilization of specialized resources across a number of projects increased in importance. Firms worked to avoid duplication of personnel or fractional utilization of shared resources. Internally, the need to increase utilization caused the functional managers to regain some of their previous strengths. Reduced size increased the importance of the utilization of resources and of its champion, the resource manager.

This brief account of the aerospace industry demonstrates the effect of environmental influences upon internal decision processes. Normally, the general manager would watch these trends and alter decision-making behavior accordingly. When decisions are decentralized, however, the general managers must change internal power bases as well as their own decision behavior. The task of the general manager is then to see that the distribution of internal influence reflects the external realities faced by the organization. The general manager must therefore take an open system view of the organization (Galbraith 1973, 117–18).

RESOURCE ALLOCATION PROCESSES

Organizations undertake a myriad of activities in allocating their resources. These activities are usually labeled as budgeting, planning, and control processes. (For an extensive discussion of the design and control of such formal systems, see Lorange [1980] or Lorange, Scott Morton, and Ghoshal [1986] from this series.) These are the processes that Rumelt and Williamson suggested were responsible for the superior performance of the multidivisional firm in managing diversity. Although a great deal of scholarly attention has been devoted to the methods of allocating resources rationally from an economic viewpoint, equally important is understanding that decisions are the product of organizational and political processes.

Toward that end, Cyert and March's *Behavioral Theory of the Firm* served as a point of departure (1963). The behavioral theory was intended to introduce a better description of how decisions were actually made rather than how they should be made. The authors indicate that if one introduces cognitive limits of human beings, together with uncertainty and lack of agreement over goals, then the actual processes are quite different from those prescribed by management scientists. Cyert and March's work prompted others to view resource allocation not as single choices but as organizational processes. For instance, determining who made a specific decision or when that decision was made is usually difficult in retrospect. Aharoni (1966) found that no one investment decision is made at a specific point in time. Rather, the process is long, is spread over a considerable period of time, and involves many people at different echelons of various departments. Throughout this process, numerous "subdecisions" have to be made. These subdecisions usually reduce the degrees of freedom of the decision-making unit and therefore influence the final outcome of the process (Aharoni 1966, 35).

Further, in some situations, in contrast to the rational economic model, the decision to invest is made by someone in the organization. The information is then collected and analyses are performed to tailor the request to the interests of top management and the chosen strategy.

A specific examination of the resource allocation process in a large diversified company, conducted by Bower (1970), provides further elaboration of this process. He distinguished three sequential steps that took place at three different levels of the organization. First was the definition phase at the department level, where the need for investment was recognized and a proposal created to reduce a discrepancy. Next, the proposal was given impetus when a division manager bought it and agreed to back it and commit him- or herself to it. Finally was the approval by corporate management in the allocating of scarce funds. Bower's work is a thorough description of this process for four investments. He, too, was interested in describing the actual process and in distinguishing it from more quantitative but naive versions of investment decisions. No attempt was made by Bower or by the other researchers previously mentioned to distinguish variations in the process and to relate them to variations in strategy.

Strategy and Resource Allocation Processes

Bower's study provides a useful framework from which meaningful recommendations regarding resource allocation decisions can be made that account for the complexities of strategy and structure. Note, however, that resource allocation decisions are not limited to capital investments only, but include decisions regarding all resources, be it personnel for technology development or managerial skill.

Contrasts can be made in the locus of decision-making authority and involvement in various types of firms. As Akerman (1970) has described, in vertically integrated companies, all three of Bower's levels are active in the definition phase of new investments, with any of the three suggesting the need for a new project. As such, the corporate level of integrated firms is typically involved in risk assessment, economic analyses, and strategic assessments iteratively with division management. This adoption of a centralized process for capital alllocation is appropriate in vertically integrated firms where high interdependence exists among various organizational entities. In the case of an integrated oil company, capital allocation decisions for exploration and production, refining, and marketing and distribution outlets must each take into account how they will affect the rest of the company. The corporate level then serves as a clearinghouse for information and must be centrally involved at all decision points. This is possible because the corporate level typically has an element of knowledge and competence regarding the business of the firm. These firms are typically the upstream capital-intensive companies.

Multidivisional firms must address resource allocation in a different way. According to Williamson (1975), the formation of independent "natural" business units in the multidivisional form creates units from which profit can be measured and across which funds can be transferred. The multidivisional form can identify and audit substandard performance, and remove inferior management more easily than the capital market could if the units operated independently. These measurement and audit features lead Williamson to propose that resources are more likely to be used optimally (in a profit maximizing way) in the multidivisional firm when it is faced with large and diverse businesses.

Correspondingly, the finding has been that in diversified companies, investment proposals are initiated at the department level (Akerman 1970). During the impetus phase, however, division management makes the primary analysis of risk and return. The corporate level may heavily rely on the division management, using selection of that manager and subsequent accountability for performance as the means of control, and viewing budget numbers as a contract to which the division commits itself.

The degree of decentralization within the resource allocation process for multidivisional firms must be specifically designed, however, in light of the firms' overall diversity and size. Unrelated diversified firms, which pursue broadly diverse product-market positions, should employ highly decentralized resource allocation processes, as they cannot develop the capability to effectively analyze investment proposals across a range of industrial and environmental settings. The key capability of such firms, which typically grow by acquisition, rests in their ability to attract and retain acquired managers who themselves possess expertise in newly entered fields. They are then given high division autonomy, financial backing, general management coaching, and performance targets. However, such firms must also utilize sophisticated financial planning and control information systems to closely monitor performance (Berg 1965; Dundas and Richardson 1982).

Related diversified firms must actively and effectively exploit opportunities for resource sharing either within existing domains or in the development of new domains. This necessitates a greater involvement above the division level in investment and allocation decisions. This usually translates to the creation of functional staffs at the corporate level, who influence not only resource-based decisions but also functional policies. In some cases, firms grow to a size where introducing groups as a level between the divisions and the corporate office is appropriate. For example, this has been done by General Electric (which calls them sectors) and by TRW. This is especially employed when relatedness is high among a group of divisions to the extent that interdivisional sharing of some resources, such as manufacturing or research facilities, is possible. For large related diversified firms, high performance is associated with the focus of power and influence for resource allocation at the group rather than at the corporate level (Nathanson 1980). Smaller related diversified firms must execute a more active role at the corporate level, as the group level is unnecessary.

Center of Gravity and Resource Allocation Processes

Not only should the role of various levels and structural entities be matched to strategy for purposes of resource allocation decisions, but also specific resource allocation processes may be more critical in some settings than in others. In this regard, the concept of center of gravity, developed in Chapter 4, emerges as a helpful construct. As stated, upstream and downstream companies are very different. This difference extends to internal processes. The upstream companies, in the business of raw material development and commodity processing, are heavily capital intensive and therefore almost by definition are driven by the capital budgeting process. The downstream companies also have capital budgets, but depending on how far downstream, one may find other internal processes more strategic in character.

For example, those firms with a center of gravity as a product producer, such as 3M, Hewlett-Packard, or Corning Glass Works, must give particular attention to the R&D budget. This is not to suggest that all firms at this center of gravity will adopt the same

R&D posture. Indeed, some will strive to be innovators or pioneers, being first to the market with proprietary technology or product positions. Others may well decide to be followers, stressing imitation of early market entrants and product design for efficiency of manufacturing. Therefore, R&D investment will reflect the firm's particular business-level strategy (Maidique and Patch 1982). Nonetheless, R&D decisions are critical to all firms in this category. As a contrast to this, upstream firms invest in R&D, but typically emphasize process development and field support to lower costs.

Moving downstream, other processes become more important. For firms that are marketers, such Procter and Gamble, General Mills, or R. J. Reynolds, the advertising budget assumes a strategic character as it becomes a prime vehicle in support of the firm's key task, which is to sell. Finally, retail firms at the extreme upstream position find that inventory control and the management of accounts receivable are extremely important.

This is not to suggest that other processes do not play a role. Clearly, exclusive focus on advertising by a firm with a center of gravity as a marketer, without adequate and careful attention to product development and facilities planning, would be ill-advised. Nonetheless, some of these processes assume a more strategic nature than others according to center of gravity, as they are closer to the key success factors of that category.

INFORMATION SYSTEMS

A key tool of management, both for purposes of assessing resource allocation choices and for monitoring ongoing performance, is the firm's formal management information system. Such a system, in contrast to the financial reporting for external audiences (investors, regulatory bodies, and so on), is designed to directly support internal managerial decision making. Although it should be particularly obvious that such systems must reflect strategy, in situations of strategic change, their role is particularly heightened.

New technologies associated with computer-based MIS, such as data base management, will move toward greater flexibility of systems, but at present, most firms must choose the type and form of information to be collected and reported. Parsimony becomes important, as in many situations, managers suffer from a general overload of information.

Looking at type of strategy, most single-business and dominant-business firms tend to structure their systems around cost centers, where most managers are functional specialists and manage to a cost budget. Total profitability is integrated at the corporate level. Dominant-product firms, which are diversified into a few smaller businesses that constitute a fraction of total operations, must usually develop both cost and profit center accounting systems. In such settings, interdependence with the core business requires the use of allocation systems and internal transfer prices.

Multidivisional firms, however, are typically organized into a number of divisions, each of which constitutes a profit center. As such, management information systems focus on product or market division profit-and-loss statements. Degree of relatedness presents a difficulty here as well, however. Related diversified firms that typically share resources must allocate costs across divisions, whereas unrelated diversified firms that comprise virtually discrete businesses can develop truly independent financial statements.

Little disagreement exists regarding the prior explication. However, in situations of strategic shift, MIS becomes a tool by which the firm begins to assess the advisability of a new strategy or, once embarked upon, its success in the early stages.

This point can best be emphasized by an example. A multibank corporation operated for a number of years as a true holding company with each bank independently structured and managed. Further, each bank developed its own strategy for its locality, directed toward maximizing its individual profitability. The MIS for the corporation was a compilation of individual entity statements. By the early 1980s, however, with deregulation and the advent of an increasingly competitive marketplace for financial services, the corporation contemplated a strategic shift that included a more centrally driven product-market strategy, where key choices would be: In which banking and bank-related businesses would the firm compete, and how would it compete in those businesses?

This required, as part of a strategic planning process, the definition of the businesses in which the corporation presently competed and how profitable these businesses were. As the existing MIS was structured differently, around profitability of individual banks, data to support these analyses were not immediately available, taking time and resources to amass. Once the advisability of such a strategy was determined, greater refinement of the new information systems was necessary to support effective implementation of the new strategy. As a result, a number of months were required to develop a fully supportive system once the strategic shift had been decided upon, resulting in forced "blind flying" early on.

This example points to the advisability of using formal information systems of the firm as one of the mechanisms employed early to aid diagnosis and strategic change. As external analysis and other activities of the planning process suggest change, ad hoc data collec-

5

3

tion and analysis result. As a new strategy emerges and is institutionalized, the management information systems should be tailored to match it. In this fashion, formal information systems, along with reward systems (as discussed in Chapter 6) are among the first variables matched with strategy, in most cases well before a new organization structure can be designed and implemented.

SUMMARY AND MANAGERIAL IMPLICATIONS

In this chapter, we were concerned with the integrating process used to cope with general management problems that are associated with various product-market strategies. This issue is important, because the most effective firms are those that differentiate their functions to the extent needed to adapt to functional subenvironments, while simultaneously finding mechanisms to integrate these differentiated functions (Lawrence and Lorsch 1967). These integrating mechanisms provide a means of dealing with issues relating to the overall corporate environment.

A number of specific mechanisms, then, are used to achieve this interdepartmental coordination. They range from hierarchical referral to the creation of product management departments. These mechanisms increase in cost and also in their ability to cope with uncertainty and diversity as one moves toward the product management departments. The organization must choose from this ordered list of mechanisms.

Organizations pursuing strategies characterized by interdepartmental activity, high uncertainty, and high diversity will select mechanisms farther down the list (closer to integrating departments) than will organizations pursuing strategies characterized by low uncertainty and diversity.

Also, each step down the list of coordinating mechanisms represents a step toward a more product-oriented structure. Therefore, the change from a functional to a product structure need not be a major discrete alteration but can be an evolutionary movement. The point at which product and function are of equal power is called a matrix organization. The choice for the organizer becomes whether to give priority to product or to function. Factors favoring a move to the product side include diversity, new product introductions, increasing interdependence among functional departments, and an increased need for responsiveness to markets. However, the organization must be large enough to achieve economies of scale in production. The factors that favor remaining with a functional organization include the economy of scale factor, the need for special expertise, and the need for career paths for specialists.

Current thinking regarding resource allocation processes suggests that the cognitive limits of decision makers, uncertainty, and a lack of agreement over goals (Cyert and March 1963) produce behaviors very different from the view of classical economists and management scientists. Research indicates that an investment decision is the result of a long process involving a number of individuals at different levels of the organization and many subdivisions that can serve to reduce the degrees of freedom of the decision-making unit. The argument has been made that the prime locus of decision making for purposes of resource allocation should be matched to the strategy of the firm.

Formal management information systems serve as a tool for both planning and control. Although the need to tailor such systems to the firm's strategy is understood, their importance increases under conditions of strategic change.

From the topics addressed in this chapter, a number of managerial implications emerge:

1. Firms must match integrating processes to the degree of diversity and uncertainty which reflect strategy and environmental choices. As discussed previously, organizations create integrating mechanisms to cope wih general management problems of interdepartmental coordination caused by product and market diversity. The mechanisms, such as product task forces, are information and decision processes that are general manager substitutes but are less than full-time equivalents that result from product divisionalized structures. These mechanisms vary in their cost and in their ability to cope with uncertainty and diversity. The more diversity in the business strategy, the greater the number of mecchanisms adopted. For diverse and uncertain strategies, separate roles are created around the sources of diversity. These roles, such as product management roles, represent the move to matrix structures, in which, for example, the organization is simultaneously product and functional oriented.

The power and value of these integrating processes are such that if carefully designed in conjunction with management information systems and reward systems (to be discussed in Chapter 6), they can allow a firm to retain the economies of scale and other benefits of a functional organization, while attaining a necessary product-market focus of a diversified firm, without reorganizing. This is typically the case with smaller firms embarking on related diversification or with firms of any size that must give emphasis to more than one organizing element: function, product, market, geography, and so on.

2. Matrix organizational forms are typically transitional in character and require certain top management attention.   The matrix is not the ultimate structure but, like all structures, is a transitional one that should be adopted when conditions merit, and discarded when conditions no longer pertain. Second, simultaneous structures are flexible structures that can be adjusted and fine tuned by altering the power distribution of the existing roles as strategy and environment change. Less need exists for the wrenching reorganizations such as General Motors experienced as described by Chandler (1962). Third, the task of the chief executive is one of power balancing. The power balance among the roles needs to be adjusted continually with regard to assignments, salary, physical location, titles, and other factors. Thus, as technological changes such as minicomputers reduce economies of scale and promote power shifts to self-contained product divisions, chief executives need to plan the organization as they plan strategy and investments. The internal power distribution must produce decisions consistent with external reality and strategy.

3. The locus of decision-making authority (and, by extension, staff support) for resource allocation must match the firm's strategy.   As described, a number of steps are within the resource allocation process, described by Bower to include definition, impetus, and approval. Ultimately, top management must approve all resource allocation decisions, but they face a range of options regarding their own involvement in definition and impetus, and how much they will rely upon lower levels in the approval process itself. Correspondingly, the definition for many projects of a functional or operational character emerges from departments of an individual business or division. Other definitions of a more strategic character, such as proposed acquisitions, may emanate from either the division or the corporate levels.

Overall, the diversity of the firm influences how such processes should operate. Single-business and vertically integrated firms require active corporate involvement in all three of Bower's steps, given their role as coordinators of interdependent functional units or integrated operating divisions. Unrelated diversified firms delegate certainly the definition and impetus stage, and should rely heavily upon the recommendations of division managers in approving resource allocation decisions, as corporate management lacks adequate operating knowledge of widely diverse businesses. In this case, resource allocations are part of a performance contract that is monitored through sophisticated information and financial planning systems. Related diversified firms must exploit opportunities for interdivisional synergy. As such, the corporate office must be actively involved in both the impetus and the approval stages. For larger, related diversified firms, this might best be done at the group level, which is a level of structure between the division and corporate office that captures highly related divisions that, in many cases, share a number of resources.

4. Internal processes will differ in strategic importance according to the firm's center of gravity.   As discussed in Chapter 4, the character of upstream and downstream firms differ strongly, for the most part due to differences in the competencies and required success factors that emerge from their primary task orientations. The capital budgeting process is a driving factor for a natural-resource-based firm, while advertising budgeting is virtually nonexistent. In contrast, the determination of the size and allocation of the advertising budget for a downstream marketer of products may well represent the most critical resource allocation decision of the firm.

Given that the strategic importance of various internal processes will differ from firm to firm according to center of gravity, top management must consciously and explicitly identify those that are more important to the firm. The design of those processes must be examined to ensure that the right individuals, by position and level in the organization, are adequately involved at various steps of the process. The objective is to match top management time and attention to the importance of particular internal processes.

5. Management information systems must reflect intended and emerging strategy as well as existing strategy.   As a tool for both planning and control, formal management information systems are a necessary ingredient to the firm's ability to assess the appropriateness of strategic change as well as the success of a new strategy as it unfolds. For this reason, MIS should be one of the first tools that management alters in the face of strategic change. Indeed, data gathered and analyzed may lead to decisions to increase or decrease the rate of change or to revert to the old strategy. In such change situations, formal information systems provide new or additional focus for managers on what is a priority. Changes in these systems, although not cost free, are more readily reversible, whereas changes in other managerial variables, such as structure and reward systems, are more lasting in impact and less reversible in the short run.

6

Strategy, People, and Rewards

No strategy is ever implemented without capable, motivated people from the key decision makers of the firm down through those at the operational and technical levels of the organization whose specific actions move the firm toward attaining its goals. This chapter investigates the design of reward systems, with particular attention given to reward systems for top managers, and their relation to strategy. Further, we consider issues of assessing general management traits required for specific strategies, as well as how to develop adequate managerial depth to support the firm's strategic direction and posture.

REWARD SYSTEMS

One of the most important and potent components of organization is the mechanism by which performance is measured, evaluated, and rewarded. Quite simply, this is because the actual reward systems of the firm do focus and influence individual behavior. The study of the motivating value of various reward and punishment schemes has been a major research activity of organization behavior specialists for some time. Although the primary concern for purposes of strategy implementation is the reward system for senior managers, the conceptual and research foundations in this area concentrate on lower- and middle-level personnel. Note that knowledge of such research is relevant to senior managers in designing reward systems for lower-level individuals who ultimately implement all operational activities of the firm that must be linked to strategy.

A broad summary of research on rewards, and compensation in

particular, is offered by Lawler (1977). He argues that research confirms the conventional wisdom that when pay is tied to performance, it motivates higher performance. Despite its obviousness, this view is not unanimous (Meyer 1975). We also observe, however, that reward systems must be viewed as broadly composed of direct monetary compensation, benefit packages and associated perquisites, bonus incentive plans, promotion and career development opportunities, and managerial praise and recognition, as well as intrinsic rewards emanating from job satisfaction.

Lawler's work has also led to a typology of the different kinds of pay plans and their likely motivational consequences. First, money rewards can be given as salary increases or bonuses. The reward can be given on the basis of individual, group, or organization-wide performance. Second, performance can be measured by productivity or profit, by cost effectiveness or cost reduction, or by a superior's rating. Lawler rates these pay plans according to their ability to tie pay to performance, to produce dysfunctional side effects (such as encouraging short-run performance at long-run expense), to encourage cooperative behavior between people, and to promote employee acceptance.

This typology leads to specific choices whose trade-offs become evident. For example, individual bonuses based on productivity or profit are best at linking pay and performance, but have the strongest relation to side effects and are weakest at encouraging cooperation. If managers want to reduce side effects, they do so at the expense of the pay-performance-individual initiative relation. The more one opts for global and cooperative plans, the more ambiguous the individual "pay for performance relation." The last point raised by Lawler is the concept of system congruence. That is, there is no single best reward system. An effective system depends on the organization's task and strategy, and on the fit of that reward system with the organization's structure, processes, and other systems.

One of the earliest considerations of the linkage between compensation policy and strategy was developed and elaborated by Salter (1973). When considering incentive or bonus compensation for group and division executives, several choices are available. First, there is a choice of financial instruments such as cash, stock, deferred cash, and several others. Second, there is the choice of performance measure and the amount of discretion in allocating the rewards. Finally, the amount of bonus is considered. In choosing a plan, Salter suggests that management analyze the strategy to examine the appropriate time horizon of the decision maker (short-run versus long-run), the amount of risk taking to encourage, the degree of cooperation with other managers that is required, and the likely difference between corporate and divisional goals. The results of Salter's analysis are shown in Table 6.1. His recommendations, which are generally consistent with those of Lawler, have provided management with some basis for designing reward policies.

In recent years, however, as firms have more consciously managed with an eye toward strategy, several pertinent and supportable criticisms have emerged regarding the design of incentives for top management. Rappaport (1983) raises three basic concerns. First is the observed correlation of increased pay for senior managers with increased firm size. Here, he observes that increased size is not per se better in that economic value is created only when the company invests at a risk-adjusted rate of return greater than that demanded by investors in the securities market.

Second, short-term performance has until recently been heavily emphasized, oftentimes at the direct expense of long-term strategic developmental programs (Lorange 1980). This is often cited as a key contributing factor in the loss of competitive advantage to foreign competitors in such base industries as steel and automobiles. As will be discussed next, firms are increasingly adopting multiyear reward mechanisms, but in many cases fewer than one-third of bonus recipients within the firm are included in the long-term plans. Additionally, the bonus for annual performance is typically larger than that for long-term performance (Rappaport 1978).

Third, firms typically rely heavily on managerial accounting measures of performance—earnings per share, return on investement, or absolute profit and related trends and comparisons—rather than by performance measures that reward for the creation of economic value to the shareholders. In stating that the issue is not one of pay for performance, but rather "pay for what performance?" Rappaport argues that

> earnings growth can be achieved not only when management is investing at a rate of return above that demanded by the market, but also when it is investing below the market rate and thereby decreasing the value of the common shares. This is the case because the earnings figure does not reflect changes in risk or changes in expectations about inflation nor does it take into account the incremental working capital and fixed investment needed to grow the business— all critical parameters in establishing economic value. In fact, many companies achieved impressive double digit, annual earnings per share growth rates during the 1970's while providing their shareholders minimal or negative rates of return from dividends plus share price changes. In sum the problem associated with performance measurement is not only the undue emphasis on the short term, but also the more fundamental problem of measurements based on an inappropriate bottom line. (Rappaport 1983, 50)

Table 6.1 Key Aspects of Incentive Compensation

Policy Issues	Financial Instruments	Performance Measures	Degree of Discretion in Allocating Bonus Awards	Size and Frequency of Awards
Short-run vs. long-run	Mix of current bonus awards and stock options should reflect the relevant time horizon for policy-level executives. Deferred instruments are weak reinforcers of short-term performance.	Mix of quantitative measures of performance and more qualitative measures should reflect the relevant time horizon for executives. Qualitative measures usually reflect long-run considerations more effectively than quantitative measures.	Nondiscretionary, formula-based bonuses tend to encourage a short-run point of view.	Frequent bonus awards encourage concentration on short-term performance.
Risk aversion vs. risk taking	Current bonus awards, in cash or stock, can reinforce risk-taking behavior.	Qualitative measures of performance can reinforce initiative by assuring executives that total performance will be evaluated for purposes of bonus awards.	Completely discretionary, highly personalized bonuses do not clarify the "rules of the game" and as a result can discourage risk-taking behavior.	The size of both salary and incentive awards should be commensurate with the business and personal risks involved.
Interdivisional relationships		Bonus pools can be based on divisional performance, total corporate performance, or some mix of the two. Each arrangement sends different signals in terms of interdivisional cooperation.	Nondiscretionary, formula-based bonuses for division managers are most practical in companies where little cooperation among divisions is required. Discretionary bonuses are practical when top management wants to encourage cooperation among divisions.	

(continued on next page)

Table 6.1 Key Aspects of Incentive Compensation (continued)

Policy Issues	Financial Instruments	Performance Measures	Degree of Discretion in Allocating Bonus Awards	Size and Frequency of Awards
Company-division relationships	Stock options can effectively link the interests of division personnel to the interests of the corporation.	Use of objective measures of performance for division managers is more meaningful where the primary role of headquarters is to allocate capital than it is in instances where the head office plays an important role in "managing the business" of the divisions.	Nondiscretionary, formula-based bonuses are most practical in companies where headquarters does not interfere in management of the profit centers. Discretionary bonuses are most useful when top management wants to exert a direct influence on decisions in the divisions.	

Source: Malcolm S. Salter, "Tailor Incentive Compensation to Strategy," *Harvard Business Review*, March—April 1973, Copyright © 1973 by the President and Fellows of Harvard College; all rights reserved.

A fourth criticism of established practice is offered by Norburn and Miller (1981). They argue that portfolio concepts of corporate strategy, as exemplified by the Boston Consulting Group or the General Electric matrices (see Hofer and Schendel [1978]), specifically differentiate a firm's various business units along strategic dimensions, while managerial and control systems do not typically reflect variations expected according to portfolio placement. Firms continue to employ the managerial accounting measures referenced earlier, in many instances anticipating performance on a trend line that steadily increases. However, portfolio theory is explicitly predicated on the observation that some businesses can be expected to increase in profitability, while others will not. Some may sacrifice profitability for increased market share, while others may in fact decrease in profitability as the business is harvested.

In response to these criticisms, new approaches to rewarding senior management have emerged.

Extended Long-Term Performance Evaluation Periods. In response to the issue of short-term orientation, a number of firms have adopted plans that compensate top management for achieving certain performance levels over several years (usually three to five) rather than just one (Rappaport 1981; Stonich 1981). Additionally, such goal-planning horizons are moving, since new goals are established for an additional year as each year passes. In this way, the executive continually faces a new set of long-term goals. Corporate-level managers are typically awarded deferred stock or options according to a formula based on attaining various strategic goals or earnings growth targets. Division-level managers typically receive bonuses linked to divisional goals. Termed "golden handcuffs" by some, these systems reinforce managerial stability by allowing top managers to build a personal financial base that increases with time, while they also stretch their decision-making time horizon.

Weighted Strategic Factors Approach. Recognizing the lack of uniformity in the strategic position of various business units within a diversified firm, the weighted strategic factors method allows for the identification of various factors related to future profitability, which are subsequently incorporated into incentive packages and against which performance is assessed (Rappaport 1981; Stonich 1981). Examples might include market share, productivity, product quality, or new product development. For comparability across SBUs within one firm, four to five major factors might be selected, and then each is weighted differently in the determination of the individual manager's bonus. For example, a firm may select four strategic factors: return on assets, cash flow, progress against plan on identified strategic projects, and market share. A manager of a high-growth business might then be rewarded a bonus based on these four factors weighted 10%, 0, 45%, and 45%, respectively, while a manager of a low-growth business would receive a bonus weighted 50%, 50%, 0, and 0 (Stonich 1981, 349).

Strategic Funds Deferral.   Strategic funds deferral is a mechanism that encourages managers to view developmental expenses as different from expenses to sustain current operations (Stonich and Zaragoza 1980). This is accomplished by calculating return on assets for current operations only. Investments associated with strategic projects, typically included in such calculations, are separated out. This allows for the separate consideration of funds expended in the generation of current revenues and those invested in the future of the business, and associated performance against each.

A related approach to this method is what Rappaport (1978) terms the management accounting approach, which calls for the use of accounting approaches that primarily consider motivational implications and internal decision making in contrast to the use of financial accounting systems, which are used in reporting to stockholders and regulatory bodies. For example,

> consider the case of R&D expenditures. Financial accounting standards dictate immediate expensing of all R&D outlays. To encourage executives to take reasonable business risks, the management accounting approach could call for capitalizing certain outlays and expensing them gradually in subsequent periods. Alternatively, profit might be calculated before R&D; thereby the evaluation of development costs would be separated from current operations. (Rappaport 1978, 85)

Economic Value Creation Performance Measures.   As mentioned earlier, the use of accounting-based performance measures can lead to the reinforcement of behaviors not in the best interests of the stockholders. Toward this end, Rappaport (1981, 1983) has suggested a mechanism that facilitates both the selection of specific strategies from among various alternatives as well as the assessment of performance and subsequent rewards of top managers. In brief, this calls for the estimation of future cash flows associated with each strategy and the assessment of economic value to stockholders of alternative strategies at the business unit as well as at the corporate level. (For detailed discussions, see Rappaport [1981].) The planned shareholder value contribution of the adopted strategy can then be compared with the actual shareholder value contributed for purposes of performance appraisal.

Application of these emerging mechanisms or combinations

thereof can be expected to more closely integrate the firm's strategy to its managerial reward system, a linkage that has been lacking in a number of firms. Although the ability to tailor these mechanisms to the various requirements of corporate- and division-level strategy is implicit here, it is not expressly addressed for all of them. Further, the specific strategy of the firm regarding the degree of diversification complicates the design of reward systems across levels. We turn to this issue in the next section.

Rewards and Diversification

Some researchers have compared reward system variations with strategy and structure variation. Berg (1969) credits the conglomerate with motivating managers rather than coordinating them. The interdependence and need for cooperation between divisions are eliminated, and managers are rewarded generously on the basis of financial performance, usually with equity compensation. Thus, they are encouraged to take risks, to take a short- and long-term view, and to balance division versus corporate goals. Cooperation is voluntary and encouraged only if it pays off for the division.

Lorsch and Allen (1973) also compared the performance evaluation systems of their sample of diversified and vertically integrated companies. Their results are consistent with the results of Akerman (1970) and Berg (1965), and the hypotheses of Williamson (1975). The diversified companies rewarded division managers against explicit a priori goals. Rewards were tied directly to the accomplishment of end results. The pool of funds from which rewards were given resulted directly from division profits against the budget. In contrast, division performance evaluation for integrated firms was more informal and was not explicitly related to profit. There was no formula for determining bonus awards, and management exercised more discretion in awarding year-end incentive compensation.

The diversified companies placed more emphasis on "end-result" criteria, whereas integrated firms used both end-result and operating and intermediate measures. The more informal approach and the larger number of measures were possible for the integrated firms because they pursued less diverse strategies, faced less uncertain environments, and operated more interdependent technologies. Also, corporate and division managers had greater contact. Alternatively, the diversified companies had more self-contained divisions that facilitated intraorganizational causation analyses, faced more diverse and uncertain tasks, and explicitly measured end-result performance. Thus, the study explicitly linked monetary compensation for the diversified companies but not for the integrated ones.

These results are largely consistent with a more recent empirical study by Kerr (1985). In a study of twenty firms, detailed data were collected regarding the nature of rewards and strategy. Strategy was operationalized using Rumelt's (1974, 1977) categorical scheme as well as by using Leontiades (1980) designation of evolutionary versus steady-state growth patterns. Evolutionary largely describes firms that are externally oriented and grow by acquisition, while steady-state firms are committed to a core business or businesses and tend to grow by internal development. Kerr's findings strongly suggest two ideal types of reward systems: hierarchical and performance based.

Hierarchical systems were those that evaluate and reward based upon the perceptions and judgments of superiors. They equally weight qualitative and quantitative measures, which were not necessarily strongly linked to strategic mission but were driven by corporate-level performance. Bonuses in the systems typically constituted 30 percent of salary or less. Further, such systems stressed promotion from within and interfunctional as well as interdivisional transfers. Such systems were moderately associated with higher degrees of relatedness in their diversification strategy and strongly associated with the mode of diversification—steady state (internal development).

This finding makes sense, as these firms are characterized by high degrees of interdependence between corporate and division levels and across divisions. Correspondingly, Kerr argues that hierarchical reward systems can be seen as compatible with the support of the existing business, the need for close coordination and control, and a long-term perspective. Such systems can be seen to motivate behaviors rather than outcomes while developing managers with a systemwide perspective and detailed knowledge of the business.

In contrast, performance-based reward systems are more precise, objective, and quantitative in their orientation and are strongly tied to individual business unit performance. Bonuses here can account for potential salary increments of from 40 percent to an unlimited amount. This performance-based system was moderately associated with strategies of increased unrelatedness, but was strongly associated with the evolutionary mode of diversification (acquisition). Kerr argues in this instance that this comprises an appropriate fit as well. Such firms typically are less committed to the existing businesses. More importantly, the corporate-level managers may not have the intimate knowledge of each business unit to evaluate the performance of managers. The adoption of a few common denominators comparable across divisions (and appropriately weighted as previously discussed) allows for effective performance appraisal and resource allocation decisions. Additionally, as managers in diversified firms may be largely autonomous, with little interdependence to the corporate level or the other divisions beyond funds flow, such systems can be used to reward independent entrepreneurial and innovative activities appropriate to such settings.

PEOPLE AND CAREERS

As a number of authors have noted (Kotter 1982; Tichy, Fombrun, and Devanna 1982; Gupta 1984), different strategies present different general management (GM) tasks. More specifically, knowledge, skills, and the personality and manager traits required of top managers will differ according to the competitive and developmental status of the firm. Therefore, a reasonable argument is that effective strategy implementation is predicated, at least in part, upon attaining a good match between the skills, attitudes, and practices of general managers and the competitive settings that they face.

A primary approach to this people dimension of strategy implementation originally emanated from consulting firms selling strategy-related support services to multidivisional firms. The primary approach was to match the GM to a product or market division according to its particular stage of the product life cycle or according to its portfolio placement.

Some corporations are beginning to move in this direction. Tichy, Fombrun, and Devanna (1982) cite examples of firms that actively attempt to match the characteristics and skills of the general manager to the strategy of the unit. More specifically, the authors note that General Electric has employed the notion of developing and placing "growers" for wildcat or question mark businesses, "defenders" for star businesses, "harvesters" for cash cows, and "undertakers" for dog business. A second example offered by these authors is that of Corning Glass Works, "where an extensive effort is underway to assess the company's top 100 executives for such qualities as entrepreneurial flair. The goal is to have a clearer profile of the company's pool of executive talent specified in terms of capabilities for managing different parts of the BCG matrix" (Tichy, Fombrun, and Devanna 1982, 52). Chase Manhattan Bank and Texas Instruments are said to be moving in a similar direction.

Several problems should be recognized regarding this approach. First, however appealing these ideas are, they are yet to be tested in any rigorous or analytical fashion. Second, the types of general managers are quite vague, being characterized as entrepreneurial, sophisticated manager, opportunistic milker, and so on. This vagueness can also be seen in the language in use at General Electric and elsewhere, as summarized in Table 6.2, taken from a recent review on this topic.

Table 6.2 The Normative Strategy-Manager "Fit" Literature: A Summary of Approaches Taken

Author(s)	Strategic Dimensions Examined	Terms Used for Managerial Characteristics
"Wanted: A Manager" (1980) Also Tichy et al. (1982)	SBU level only (strategic mission): Grow Defend Harvest	Growers Caretakers Undertakers
Hofer and Davoust (1977)	SBU level only (strategic mission): Invest/grow Earn/protect Harvest/divest	Mature entrepreneur Planner entrepreneur Turnaround entrepreneur Sophisticated planner Profit planner Turnaround specialist Professional manager Experienced cost cutter Professional liquidator
Leontiades (1982)	Corporate level: Steady state Evolutionary SBU level: Internal (build, hold) External (sell, buy)	Activist Growth entrepreneur Product manager R&D planner Remote controller Aloof strategist Acquiror Growth director
"The Right Manager" (1981)	SBU level only (strategic mission): Build Hold Harvest	Dimensions examined: Age Functional background Industry familiarity Length of experience
Wissema et al. (1980)	SBU level only (strategic mission): Explosion Expansion Continuous growth Consolidation Slip Contraction	Pioneer Conqueror Levelheaded Administrator Economizer Insistent diplomat
Wright (1974)	SBU level only (stage in product life cycle): Embryonic Growth Mature Aging	Entrepreneur Sophisticated market manager Critical administrator Opportunistic milker

Source: Gupta (1984), 402.

Indeed, it seems that "each of such terms has imbedded in it certain assumptions about a multiplicity of managerial characteristics including, for example, functional background, risk propensity, and interpersonal orientation" (Gupta 1984, 401).

Note that some research of a more focused type has been conducted. A number of studies have attempted to relate variations in personality to variations in management task. The first problem encountered with this kind of research is that of establishing descriptors to determine personality types. Some of the attempts to include personality in contingency theory have used tolerance for ambiguity as the basic dimension of personality that must be matched to task and structure. For the most part, people who are low in tolerance for ambiguity prefer predictable tasks and mechanistic structures (Morse and Young 1973; McCaskey 1976). People who measure high in tolerance for ambiguity prefer uncertain, changing tasks and organic structures. Another variation uses Jungian types, as measured by the Myers-Briggs indicator (Kilman and Mitroff 1976). The results are quite similar in that these authors also identify personality types that prefer various structural forms, two of which are the organic and mechanistic forms described earlier. Thus, some evidence indicates that systematic relations exist between types of people, as measured by tolerance for ambiguity; types of structure, such as mechanistic or organic; and the degree of task uncertainty.

More recent research has attempted to link managerial characteristics to strategy. Snow and Hrebiniak (1980) found a relationship between functional backgrounds and strategy operationalized in terms of firms being a "prospector," "defender," "analyzer," or "reactor." A relationship between strategy and the importance of various functions was found by Hitt, Ireland, and Palia (1982) as well. Research by Song (1982) found that marketing and product backgrounds were more prevalent among general managers of internal diversifiers, while accounting, finance, and law were more prevalent among acquisitive diversifiers. Finally, Gupta and Govindarajan (1984), in their study of managerial characteristics, strategy, and effectiveness, found that "greater marketing/sales experience, greater willingness to take risk and greater tolerance for ambiguity contribute to effectiveness in the case of build SBUs, but hamper it in the case of harvest SBUs" (p. 38). Overall, however, considerable opportunity exists for more specific and systematic development of general management traits and characteristics and their relation to successful strategy implementation.

Other questions remain as well if strategy is to serve as a prime determinant, in a strict sense, in the placement of general managers. A major element in this rationale is using stage of the life cycle as a proxy for strategy, as stage and competitive position influence portfolio placement. As Kerr (1982) points out, this entails several major assumptions: (1) It is possible to identify stage of product life cycle for a firm at any point in time; (2) we know which specific personality traits are associated with successful general management at each stage; (3) it is possible to identify such traits within individuals; and (4) there are no major social or political (or both) dysfunctions associated with changing general managers as the demands of the job change. Clearly, challenges can be offered to each of these assumptions, suggesting that a strict and technical application of the use of strategy or product life cycle stage (or both) as a contingency factor in the placement of general managers will be problematic. This then heightens the importance of the design of incentive systems for the general manager to elicit behaviors appropriate to the strategic position of the division or firm, as discussed earlier in this chapter.

Even though some impediments exist in the linkage of strategy to general management placement, the dysfunctions associated with a clear absence of this linkage should be apparent. Toward that end, it is advisable for the firm to assess four or five primary managerial traits and values, combinations of which can be seen as important. This assessment should be based upon the situation of the firm, its current product/market scope, overall stategy, and general goals and values. This approach seems to be that used by Corning Glass Works, which was described earlier. Firms can then, at least in a general, subjective fashion, consider strategy and the associated task requirements as a critical but not solitary factor in the assignment of general managers.

Management Development

The second issue relevant for this review is the focus on careers and management development. A great deal of research is focused on these topics (Campbell, Dunette, Lawler, and Weick 1970; Hall 1976; Van Maanen and Schein 1977). However, little research addresses how variations in strategies and structures are matched with variations in management development practices and career paths. Some good work is aimed at matching an individual's personal, career, and family development. So far, however, the emphasis of empirical work has been upon the individual. Macroperspectives have not been taken into consideration in empirical studies. A start in this direction is a study comparing the uses of managerial transfer in European multinational firms (Edstrom and Galbraith 1977). The authors hypothesize that large numbers of transfers of many nationalities lead to decentralized subsidiary structure.

The work of Pitts (1977) is also relevant here. He finds that firms that grow internally and presumably pursue "related diversification" strategies make use of interdivisional careers to a greater extent than do external growth firms pursuing unrelated diversification strategies. The need for technology transfer of the "related" competence is satisfied by interdivisional transfers. Similarly, most organizations that operate a mature matrix organization have career paths that encourage multidivisional and multifunctional experiences. This form of organization that arises to handle diversity while sharing resources requires generalists who know all the diverse markets, products, countries, and functions. These renaissance people are grown and developed internally by diverse sets of managerial experiences arranged through the career path. The inability to find such people is a primary limitation to the implementation of strategies of extreme diversification.

Most of this work tends to focus on the congruence of such practices with the attained strategy of the firm. However, management development systems became particularly important for firms that are in the process of changing their strategy. A major diversification or the adoption of a new strategy within the firm's existing businesses may require different skills and management practices. As a result, the firm must reconsider promotional and developmental activity so as to develop depth in required areas and to move new types of people into key positions. As an example, AT&T's move into the competitive electronic communications and knowledge business requires the development of internal promotion systems for profit-driven people who are understanding of and responsive to competitive markets. This represents a major shift from developmental systems that had stressed service with little concern for profitability or competition (Tichy, Fombrun, and Devanna 1982). Alternatively, the firm can look outside to hire new competencies or key people from the external market.

The monitoring of such developmental activities, at least for the top tier of executives of the firm, must be viewed as a strategic task. Recently, a number of firms have developed succession planning programs for upper echelon managers to ensure adequate development of individual managers and overall depth of talent to the organization.

Here again, Tichy, Fombrun, and Devanna provide examples of firms that are effective in this area. The CEO at Exxon oversees the Compensation and Executive Development Committee, otherwise composed of members of Exxon's board. The system regularly reviews the development and placement of the top 250 executives of the corporation. Meeting weekly, the group assesses future developmental needs of individuals as well as the existence of backup candidates for each of the positions discussed. Each subsidiary has a comparable system so that overall, the development and movement of the top 2,000 managers of the firm is continually planned and monitored.

At General Motors, the 6 top executives of the corporation actively review the top 600 managers with the assistance of the next level of vice-presidents and group executives. Such sessions, held twice yearly, are devoted to assessing the strengths and weaknesses of the individuals and planning out their next developmental career move. In both Exxon and General Motors, the corporation is a single-business integrated entity where general managers require broad knowledge of both the business and the industry. Correspondingly, having come up through the business, top management is in a position to assess, both subjectively and objectively, the performance and development needs of subordinates.

As a third example, General Electric, in approximately 240 separate businesses, has a succession planning and appraisal process that must be different from those just described. At General Electric, the chairman monitors the top 600 positions through a slating system. Under the direction of a senior vice-president, human resources staff specialists and line managers develop lists of acceptable candidates for key managerial positions. Promotions to these specific positions are then drawn from individuals on the slate. Although positions can be filled with individuals not on the list, such cases are viewed as exceptions requiring top-level approval and in fact are a rarity. Additionally, each year a small number of key executives, usually 40 or less, are selected for an in-depth review. Their managerial strengths, weaknesses, and accomplishments are compiled through extensive contact with superiors, subordinates, peers, and even customers. The individual is provided with an opportunity to review the report and respond to it prior to its finalization. The mechanisms of slating and in-depth reviews allow top managers of diversified corporations to make promotion and development decisions in an informed manner even though they may possess limited knowledge of the specific business in question.

People and Center of Gravity

Just as choices regarding the design of reward and career systems must consciously be matched to strategy, the firm's center of gravity also remains a consideration. The example of oil companies attempting to move to a downstream center of gravity, which was discussed in Chapter 4, makes the point. A shift downstream requires a corresponding shift in the power base of the firm away from a dominance by engineers, geologists, and refining and distribution executives toward marketing. Most likely, top management of the firm will have come up through the primary functions of the old center of gravity. To be successful in its new position, the firm must gain management talent within its upper echelon, reflective of the tasks and skills required for the new center of gravity. This will probably require the hiring of individuals from outside of the firm. In the longer run, however, it will be necessary to develop managerial depth in the new areas, through redefined career paths to top management positions and management development programs. Additionally, the degree of interdependence between levels of the organization and across divisions may change, and an increased emphasis on distinct products and their individual profitability may strongly suggest a newly structured reward system. Overall, then, center of gravity serves as an additional determinant of the reward and career systems within organizations.

SUMMARY AND MANAGERIAL IMPLICATIONS

This chapter has focused on the linkage of reward systems and human resource policies, such as placement and management development practices with strategy. After reviewing the basic elements of reward systems and their overall ties to strategy (Lawler 1977; Salter 1973), discussion centered on the design of incentives for top managers. Several problems have been observed in current practices in this area. More specifically, rewards tend to reinforce short-term orientations and do not take into account the differing strategic position of various divisions within multidivisional firms. In an effort to overcome these problems, the following approaches to rewarding senior managers are proposed:

1. Extended Long-Term Performance Evaluation Periods—which compensate top management for the achievement of certain performance levels over a multiyear time horizon
2. Weighted Strategic Factors Approach—which allows for bonus incentives tailored to various strategic positions of individual divisions of the firm
3. Strategic Funds Deferral—which employs managerial accounting practices to encourage managers to view strategic developmental expenses as different from direct operating expenses
4. Economic Value Creation Performance Measures—which reward top managers for actual contribution to shareholders' value rather than for performance against traditional accounting measures.

Finally, pertaining to rewards, the degree of diversification of the firm presents additional difficulties beyond those addressed by the weighted strategic factors approach just described. The greater the diversity of the firm, the less top management can be fully knowledgeable of all operations, and the less interdependence across divisions. As a result, more diversified firms require reward systems that are more objective, precise, and quantitative in character, and are strongly tied to individual business unit performance.

Regarding the people dimension of implementation, in both theory and practice, a match is necessary between the skills and traits of general managers and the strategic position of their divisions. Although attempts in this area to date have relied upon rather vague definitions of managerial characteristics, a strict and technical application of this idea can be problematic as well. Nonetheless, the identification of four or five managerial traits (which might include entrepreneurism, risk orientation, interpersonal skills, functional background, and others) pertinent to the firm and its setting should be identified. The match of the configuration of these traits to the strategic position of a division should then be assessed for selection and placement decisions of general managers.

Finally, management development of upper echelon managers of the firm, viewed as a strategic task of top management, must be linked to strategy. Here, diversity seems to be a factor as well, with effective single-business integrated firms using systems that rely on top management involvement with overall judgments subjectively as well as objectively derived. A more diversified firm must rely upon a more decentralized system that develops judgments regarding performance appraisal and career moves where the competence for such assessment exists. Top management must nonetheless be viewed as guardians of the system.

7

Integration of Dimensions for Strategy Implementation

Our review thus far has examined relationships between various organizational dimensions and the firm's product-market strategy. The intent was to find which structure, process, or system was most appropriate for a particular strategy. With a few exceptions, the relationships examined were between a particular organizational dimension, such as the corporate-level structure or the reward system, and strategy. However, each organizational dimension must be consistent not only with the strategy but also with the others. All the dimensions, such as structure, reward systems, and resource allocation processes, must constitute an internally consistent organizational form. Organizations are packages or mosaics in which all pieces must fit together. This concept of fit, or congruence, was raised earlier in connection with personality types. It will be raised again here because it is the key concept of organization design theory and practice.

THE CONCEPT OF FIT

The concept of fit, or congruence, among all the dimensions of the organization has emerged from several sources. Scott began talking of his stages as consisting "of a cluster of managerial characteristics" (Scott 1971, 6). In addition, he suggested that a cluster was not just an organizational form but a "way of managing," even a "way of life."

Miles and Snow (1984) see fit as "a process as well as a state—a dynamic search that seeks to *align* the organization with its environment and to *arrange* resources internally in support of that alignment. In practical terms, the basic alignment mechanism is *strategy*, and the internal arrangements are *organizational structure* and *management processes*" (p. 11) (emphasis in original). They go on to argue that perfect fit is strived for but never fully attained due to continuous changes externally. This is also the primary idea behind the seven *S*'s of strategy and organization as discussed by Waterman, Peters, and Phillips (1980), those being strategy, superordinate goals, structure, systems, style, staff, and skills.

The same notion has been elaborated by consulting firms in their own strategy and structure packages. They distinguished between products or businesses in a multidivisional firm by the stage of the product life cycle. Then they assume that the "way of managing" will vary with the stages and go on to prescribe managerial characteristics that are appropriate for the various stages. A package used by The Hay Group is shown in Table 7.1. The packages of other firms are similar, with due regard for variations in characteristics and descriptors. The main point is that *business divisions need to adopt an internally consistent set of practices in order to implement the product strategy effectively*.

Another source of development of the congruence, or fit, concept is organization theory. Leavitt was one of the first to discuss the degree to which task, structure, people, and processes form an integrated whole (Leavitt 1962, 1965). He suggests that organizational change strategies should take all dimensions into account. One cannot successfully change structure without making adjustments in compensation and reinforcing changes in information and budgeting systems, career systems, management development practices, and compensation policies. *In organizations, everything is connected to everything else.*

The major developer and empirical investigator of the fit concept has been Jay Lorsch (Lawrence and Lorsch 1967; Losch and Allen 1973; Lorsch and Morse 1974). Much of his work has already been discussed in the sections devoted to the individual dimensions. Lorsch is the primary investigator to examine structure, task, people, and administrative practices; the congruence between these dimensions; and the degree to which congruence is related to organizational performance. Those organizations that were not high performers were experiencing a situation in which either structure or process did not fit with the degree of task uncertainty.

Other research also supports the concept of fit, or congruence, as well. Findings by Child (1977) reinforce this hypothesis through his study of five international airlines and their structures and performance. In examining the two most profitable airlines, he found that they have contrasting administrative practices and structures even though they face similar problems, have similar route structures, and have equivalent sizes. But the one feature they have in common

Table 7.1 The Hay Group Strategic Issues Matrix

		Phases of Business Development			
		1. Emergence	2. Developmental	3. Mature	4. Liquidation
Characteristics	A Style Characteristics	▪Limited delegation by strong leadership ▪Variety of schemes are possible	▪Highest degree of delegation and freedom supported	▪Delegative to controlled ▪Flexibility in meeting fixed goals	▪Very limited delegation and freedom
	B Decision-Making Characteristics	▪Formalized goals virtually nonexistent ▪Information limited	▪General goals exist ▪More information for decisions	▪High degree of clarity ▪Information based Decisions	▪Rigid goals ▪Information for control
	C Planning and Control Systems Characteristics	▪Informal, highly qualitative (milestone-oriented)	▪Capable of setting broad goals and measuring results (program oriented)	▪Supportive of careful goal setting and control (P & L oriented)	▪Deemphasize long-term planning quantitative controls (balance sheet oriented)
	D Responsiveness to External Conditions Characteristics	▪Limited responsiveness at first, focus on establishing a position	▪Highly responsive ▪Adapt to market opportunities	▪Less responsiveness required due to decreasing rate of change in markets	▪Responsive but under very limited conditions

(continued on next page)

Table 7.1 The Hay Group Strategic Issues Matrix (continued)

Characteristics		Phases of Business Development			
E	Integration and Differentiation Characteristics	■ High degree of differentiation among organization units ■ Integration at top	■ Decreasing differentiation among units ■ Integrative function becoming more "local" to markets, products	■ Continuing decrease in differentiation ■ Integration "local"	■ Low differentiation ■ Integration at the top (corporate)
F	Leadership Characteristics	■ Entrepreneur, strong leader	■ Entrepreneur/business manager	■ Sophisticated manager	■ Administrator, S.O.B.
G	Motivations Characteristics	■ Venturesome ■ Accepts unaccustomed risks	■ Venturesome to conservative ■ Accustomed and unaccustomed risks	■ Conservative primarily ■ Generally risk-adverse	■ Conservative ■ Risk adverse
H	Reward Management Characteristics	■ High base compensation to attract people ■ Discretionary bonus	■ High levels related to job ■ Incentives for building results	■ More average levels related to job ■ Incentives for results above high goal	■ Average level ■ Incentives for cost control
I	Know-How and Development Characteristics	■ Know-how depth important near top ■ Development needed to support expected expansion	■ Ever broadening scope and increasing numbers of managers required	■ Development needs and know-how becoming specialized, static	■ Specialized depth and scope of know-how

Source: Reprinted by special permission of The Hay Group.

is congruence among their processes and structures. One is not divisionalized, has short time horizons, is centralized, and uses high and continuous involvement of the top management team, which meets often. It operates a personal control process and has open communications among a management cadre, which has long tenure. Conflicts are expressed and decisions are made and acted upon rapidly. The other airline has a multidivisional, regional form with decentralized profit centers. It operates with impersonal controls and sophisticated planning processes. It has a large number of administrative staff personnel who operate the impersonal control system. These observations lead Child to suggest that the consistency among these practices, structure, and people is what makes them effective.

The poor performers also had multidivisional structures for decentralization but placed restrictions on the amount of discretion that could be exercised. Although they had the structure and incurred the administrative cost of large staff overhead, they received none of the benefits of decentralization. Child's explanation of the effect of inconsistency upon performance is based on its impact on managerial behavior. The inconsistent practices give mixed signals that frustrate managers and weaken their motivation.

The most recent example of research in this area directly links organizational and management approaches with strategy. Dundas and Richardson (1980, 1982) conducted a study of performance among unrelated diversified firms. Although this strategic category of companies has consistently been found to be a low-performing one (Rumelt 1974; Nathanson and Cassano 1982), the authors nonetheless found considerable within-group variation. The logic of the unrelated diversified strategy argued by the authors in terms of the Williamson markets and hierarchies framework (discussed in Chapter 2) is that such firms can be seen as more efficient than the market in the allocation of capital across multiple investment alternatives, due to core skills in the financial area and through the form of organization they adopt, which can lower transactions costs and reduce uncertainty. More specifically, in investigating various implementation approaches associated with this strategy, they found that high performers demonstrated a strong fit between elements of strategy and organization.

Regarding strategy, Dundas and Richardson found that the successful firms typically (1) were narrowly diversified into four or five groups of businesses, each of which was somewhat comparable in terms of performance criteria; (2) had no single subsidiary comprising more than 30 percent of the total corporate portfolio; (3) owned businesses that were, or had the potential to be, industry leaders; and (4) entered into new unrelated businesses by acquisition. These strategic policies are directed at attaining an efficiency of capital allocation based upon performance of diverse businesses and a minimization of risk from poor performance by any single-business enterprise.

Regarding organizational elements, Dundas and Richardson found that the corporate offices of the successful firms were small and tended to focus on the financial/accounting, legal, acquisition, and planning functions, thus restricting operational involvement. Corporate-wide functions such as marketing, R&D, or engineering were unnecessary, given the diversity of operating businesses. Although group executives were used to facilitate span of control, operating units were kept strictly independent for several reasons. First, capital allocation and performance evaluation processes are made easier. Second, when problems arise they are easier to spot and deal with. Ultimately, if necessary, divestment decisions can be made for discrete business units. Finally, the primary performance measure and basis for rewards of divisional presidents was return on investment. Capital and cash controls were highly centralized. These are logical, since the allocation of cash and capital is the principal mechanism through which the subsidiaries are controlled.

These Dundas and Richardson findings reinforce two primary themes developed here and in earlier chapters. First, the success of any strategy is contingent, in part, on how it is implemented. Having the right strategy, by itself, is not enough. The second theme is that successful implementation emerges from the attainment of fit between the strategy and how the firm is organized and managed.

Consistent with this research, Miles and Snow (1984) have suggested that various types and degrees of fit can be observed and related to performance as follows:

- Minimal fit is required of all organizations in competitive environments.
- Tight fit is associated with long-term effectiveness.
- Early fit, which is the attainment of a new pattern of strategy and organizational linkages prior to one's competitors, can create a significant competitive advantage. (This is supported by the findings of Teece [1981] and Armour and Teece [1978], discussed in Chapter 3.)
- Fragile fit leaves the firm vulnerable to external changes and internal ineffectiveness.

Although research has been offered in support of the fit hypothesis, additional research is required. The studies cited previously are cross-sectional with small sample sizes. Even though these studies could lead to the rejection of the fit hypotheses and have not, alternative interpretations remain that cannot be rejected yet. For example, does noninvolvement of corporate offices create the autonomy that divisions use to respond to the uniqueness of their market, thereby performing at a high level? Or does high divisional performance create confidence in the minds of corporate management, who then give high-performing divisions autonomy while concentrating on the low-performing divisions? Here the cross-sectional nature of the research does not permit a rejection of the alternative explanations.

A trade-off is also involved between short-run and long-run fit. That is, the short-run congruence between all the organization design variables may be so good that they cannot be disentangled and rearranged into a new configuration in order to meet an environmental challenge or to implement a new strategy. For example, the Swiss watchmakers achieved an excellent fit between strategy and structure for the making of mechanical watches. The institutionalization of the mechanical technology has prevented these firms from adapting to the new technology. The fit is so strong that the Swiss became ready buyers from American watchmakers who wanted to dump their mechanical subsidiaries (Miles and Cameron, 1977). Overall, then, some large sample, empirical, longitudinal studies are needed to complement and reinforce this research.

A more comprehensive conceptual scheme that identifies the major design and managerial variables to be considered when matching organizational form to strategy has been developed by Galbraith (1977) and is depicted in Figure 7.1. According to this view, the product-market strategy chosen by the firm determines to a large extent the task diversity and uncertainty with which the organization must cope. The organization must then match the people with the task through selection, recruitment, and training and development practices. The people must also match the structure. The structure, also chosen to fit the task, is specified by choices of the division of labor (amount of role differentiation), the departmental structure, the shape (number of levels, spans of control), and the distribution of power (both horizontal and vertical). Across the structure, processes are overlaid to allocate resources and coordinate activities not handled by the departmental structure. These information and decision processes are planning and control systems, budgeting processes, integration mechanisms, and performance measurements. And finally, the reward system must be matched with the task and structure through choices of compensation practices, career paths, leader behavior, and the design of work. In total, all these choices must create an internally consistent design. If one of the practices is changed, the other dimensions must be altered to maintain fit. Similarly, if the strategy is changed, then all the dimensions may need to be altered so that the form of organization remains consistent with the product-market strategy.

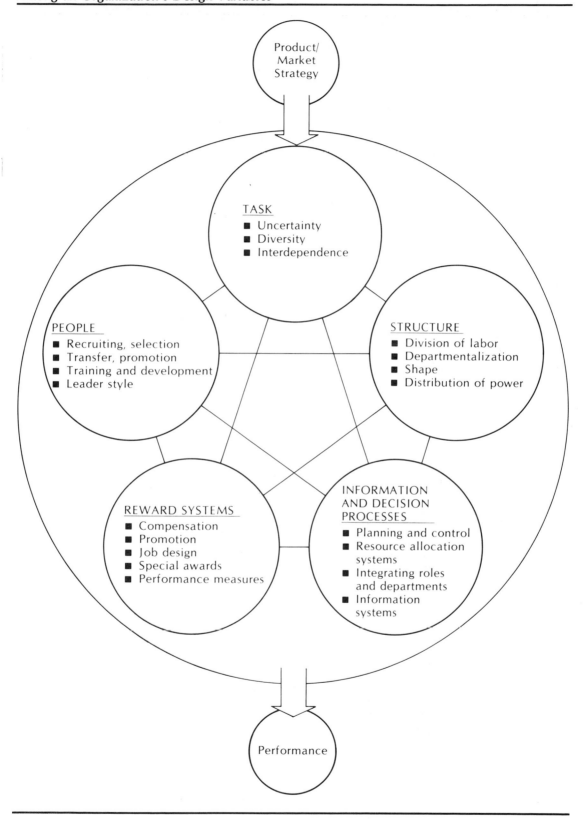

Table 7.2 Strategy-Organization Fit

Strategy	▪Dominant business ▪Vertically integrated	▪Unrelated diversified ▪Growth through acquisition	▪Related diversified ▪Growth through internal development, some acquisition
Strategic Focus and Task Focus	▪Degree of integration ▪Market share ▪Product line breadth	▪Degree of diversity ▪Types of business ▪Resource allocation across discrete businesses ▪Entry and exit businesses	▪Realization of synergy from related products, process, technologies, markets ▪Resource allocation ▪Diversification opportunities
Structure and Decision-Making Style	▪Centralized functional ▪Top control of strategic decisions ▪Delegation of operations through plans and procedures	▪Highly decentralized product divisions/profit centers ▪Small corporate office ▪No centralized line functions ▪Almost complete delegation of operations and strategy within existing businesses ▪Control through results, selection of management, and capital allocation	▪Multidivisional/profit centers ▪Grouping of highly related business with some centralized functions within groups ▪Delegated responsibility for operations ▪Shared responsibility for strategy

(continued on next page)

Table 7.2 Strategy-Organization Fit (continued)

Information and Decision Process	■Coordination and integration through structure, rules, planning, and budgeting ■Use of integrating roles for project activity across functions	■No integration across businesses ■Coordination and information flows between corporate and division levels around management information systems and budgets	■Coordinate and integrate across businesses and between levels with planning, integrating roles, integrating departments
Rewards	■Performance against functional objectives ■Mix of objective and subjective performance measures	■Formula-based bonus on ROI or profitability of divisions ■Equity rewards ■Strict objective, impersonal evaluation	■Bonus based on divisional and corporate profit performance ■Mix of objective and subjective performance measures
People and Careers	■Primarily functional specialists ■Some interfunctional movement to develop some general managers	■Aggressive, independent general managers of divisions ■Career development opportunities are primarily intradivisional.	■Broad requirements for general managers and integrators ■Career developments cross-functional, interdivisional, and corporate-divisional

Specific examples of recommended configurations of strategy and organizational variables that constitute a fit are shown in Table 7.2 for three broad strategies: single or dominant business, related diversified, and unrelated diversified.

AN EXAMPLE: DOW-CORNING

Dow-Corning has been much publicized as an organization that adopted a top-level matrix structure in the middle 1960s (Goggins 1974). Over the next decade, it had fine-tuned its structure, added additional supporting systems, and blended them into its worldwide matrix structure. Before describing that organizational form, we will give a brief description of its history and prior structure. (Note that what follows is not intended to describe the current management systems and practices at Dow-Corning. This case example does, however, reflect the tight fit between strategy and organization as of the 1970s.)

Dow-Corning is a joint venture created by Dow Chemical (50 percent) and Corning Glass (50 percent) around 1942 in order to pursue silicon-based products. From its creation until 1962, Dow-Corning was managed in an entrepreneurial start-up mode. The growing organization was coordinated through a centralized, functional structure that placed emphasis on technology and product development. Pursuing product diversification, Dow-Corning was emerging as a firm with a downstream, product producer center of gravity. The products of Dow-Corning were all related, drawing in some way upon silicon chemistry technology.

This organization grew into a $50 million business, employing 1,500 people by 1962. At that time, a sharp change in management occurred. The growth, the product diversity, and the new product development process could not be managed out of a single profit center. A new chief executive was brought in from Corning Glass to introduce a multidivisional structure consisting of five product profit centers and functional staffs with dotted-line reporting relations to the functional departments within the divisions. This change achieved integration across the functions around product application, turned around the profit situation, and continued growth.

The multidivisional structure began experiencing several problems. The expansion into international markets caused competition between domestic and foreign investments, and produced another source of diversity with which to cope. Manufacturing could not be broken apart by product, as one plant made materials for all divisions. A transfer price-investment controversy naturally arose. Much technology was applicable to all divisions but not shared during the internal competition for capital. The central research and development unit atrophied from neglect. Then, when a mini-recession hit the industry and profits fell 35 percent, a new chief executive was brought in from Dow.

In 1967, Goggins became president and began to implement the matrix on the domestic side of the organization. The five divisions were converted to ten business profit centers, each with a business manager. The functional departments reported to both the business manager and their functional vice-president. This structure is shown in Figure 7.2. This move increased the influence of the functions and

Figure 7.2 The Dow-Corning Matrix

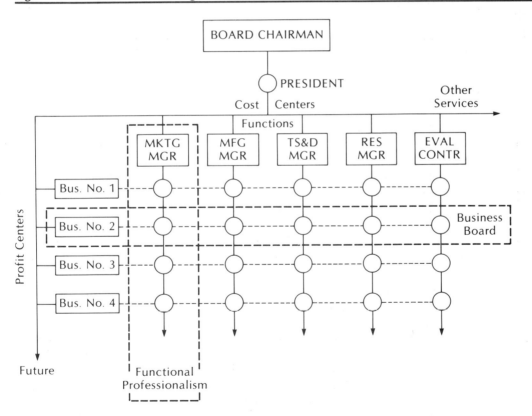

Source: William C. Goggins, "How the Multidimensional Structure Works at Dow Corning,"*Harvard Business Review,* January–February 1974. Copyright © 1973 by the President and Fellows of Harvard College; all rights reserved.

created the balance of power that characterized the matrix. The wide span of control was managed by an office of the chief executive consisting of the president and board chairman. An attempt was made to organize within the function by product as much as possible. Therefore, each business manager chaired a business board. Additionally, the subfunction managers from each function sat on the business board, which was the policy making body for that business.

In addition to the hierarchy and the ten business boards, a number of other systems and processes were used to enable the firm to continue to grow and to develop new products (30 percent of sales come from products introduced in the last five years). The products that move across the functions were assigned to business areas having a product manager and a product board. The product manager is usually a subfunction manager who wears two hats. That is, product managers manage their functional area and the new product. The board consists of representatives from the other functions. The leadership of the product boards changes with phases in the product life. Early phases are dominated by research and product development, then by manufacturing, and so on, so that the leadership moves among the subfunction managers who sit on the business board.

The dual reporting relations, two-hat product managers, and substantial new product activity all generate a good deal of cross-product and cross-functional conflict. To see that the conflict is constructively and quickly resolved, it is channeled into the planning process. Dow-Corning has the standard rolling five-year long-range plan where year one drops out as the budget. In controlling against this plan, the top group meets weekly to hear each business and function in turn. Interunit conflicts are raised and resolved. Twice a year all business groups, functional departments, and regional managers come together for three days to formulate and update the strategies and plans. The conflict is channeled into a process that leads to its resolution. The matrix generates conflict from its multiple dimensions. It is channeled into a planning process where a tie breaker exists if agreement does not naturally result. All successful matrix organizations have an effective planning process into which the conflict is channeled.

Strong emphasis is also placed on goal setting and on an MBO program. Again, the ability to work against agreed-upon goals permits a well-functioning matrix. Because people work against goals and problems rather than against each other, they have less need for hierarchy and tie breaking. (For more on MBO and related programs, see Richard's [1986] book in this series.) The MBO program requires multidimensional profit and cost reporting. As each side of the matrix needs its own information and evaluation system, a great deal of effort goes into these multidimensional information systems.

The MBO program serves as an input into the performance appraisal process. Each manager is evaluated against objectives. The subfunctional managers receive a joint evaluation from business and functional managers. Here again, the agreed-upon objectives help in reaching consensus. As in most organizations, if substantial disagreement arises the functional manager has the final say. The managers at the top also receive incentive compensation based on total company profit. Business and area managers have their own profit center, but they receive a bonus for total company profit to increase the likelihood of cooperation and effective handling of conflict. Bonuses are paid against planned profit.

The business and product boards are able to function well for other reasons. Most people selected to participate on boards have a common technical background. Almost all managers are chemical engineers. In addition, the career path is multifunctional, providing experience on both business and functional sides. This career system gives board members a sound understanding of other people's problems and facilitates general all-around communication, so that people are less concerned about territory or turf. Finally, all product and business board participants are sent to a specialized training program prior to taking a board assignment. This training in group problem solving and conflict, followed immediately by experiences utilizing the training, reinforces the ability of this organization to handle matrix conflict constructively. Thus, the selection process, the career path, and the management development practices create the people needed to make the matrix work.

The integration mechanisms were further reinforced by the physical setting, which was specifically designed for their organization. All boards are co-located in open offices, with business meeting rooms displaying business information. This arrangement gives a sense of common territory and facilitates informal day-to-day communication across functions for each business.

In summary, Dow-Corning adopted an organizational form that fit its strategy, center of gravity, and size. It pursued a strategy of product diversification, with a center of gravity based on products related to silicon chemistry. New product introduction was the key competitive issue, which required sophisticated technology, manufacturing economies of scale, and tight integration across functions. Correspondingly, R&D is seen as the critical resource allocation process. When combined with the moderate size of the business, these factors required a balance between functions and products, attained through a structure. In order to work, a matrix organization must handle conflict and cooperation across all units. The planning process, with its frequent meetings, its multidimensional profit and cost reporting, and its MBO program, plays a significant role in conflict management. It was backed up with companywide incentive compensation, business and product boards, multifunction and multibusiness careers, conflict management training, and the location of each board at the same site. The company was driven by engineers and scientists, with the career path to top management typically through research and product development. Together, these structures, systems, and processes made a successful package that worked for Dow-Corning at that stage in its development.

The purpose of the example is not to sell the matrix organization, which was not solely responsible for Dow-Corning's performance. The purpose is to discuss the fit among all the dimensions of the organization. Our belief is that the fit, along with the technology, financial policies, and other factors, was partially responsible for the successful performance. If circumstances change, such as a major increase in size, Dow-Corning should abandon the matrix. However, Dow-Corning must then achieve another fit among all its systems and processes to regain a congruence with its new strategy. This total change is what makes the transition from one stage to another so difficult. Also, this total change and the difficulty in changing have led Chandler and others to talk of stages of development and a stagewise development model. We review these and other views of strategic adaptation in Chapter 8.

SUMMARY AND MANAGERIAL IMPLICATIONS

This chapter has examined the concept of fit, or congruence, among all dimensions of organization. A number of authors have discussed the degree to which task, structure, people, and process form an integrated whole and must be consciously designed to be consistent with each other as well as with the strategy of the firm. Extending this view, Galbraith argues that the firm's product/market strategy determines the task diversity and uncertainty with which an organization must cope. The organization must also match the people with the task through selection, recruitment, training, and development. The structure, information and decision processes, and reward systems must also fit to form the integrated whole.

This chapter concluded with several recommended profiles of how organizations should be aligned to match specific strategies, and with a case example of how Dow-Corning has achieved such a fit.

Overall, this work underscores the effect of fit, or congruence, on the effectiveness of the firm. Specifically, as Miles and Snow note, some minimal level of fit is necessary for survival, and high economic performance can be associated with firms that attain a tight fit early on, thus gaining a competitive advantage. However, the nature of this strategy-organization alignment must continually be assessed, since a change in the environment, suggesting a new strategy, will require a corresponding realignment of organizational elements to regain a new congruence, but with a different configuration. Interestingly, the tighter the fit between strategy and organization, the more difficult the change process may be when it is attempted. Chapter 8 turns to these issues of strategic adaptation.

8

Strategic Adaptation Models

This chapter reviews several perspectives on how organizations change and adapt over time. The requirements for change can emerge from a number of factors linked to the firm's strategy and environment. In many instances, it involves the pursuit of growth opportunities emanating from the core business of the firm. Alternatively, the firm may be forced to respond to threats from the environment, be it declining demand or unfavorable governmental regulation. Toward this end, several perspectives of organizational development, change, and adaptation will be reviewed using (1) growth and development models, (2) a contrasting view that discusses types of organizations, and (3) the recently developed population ecology view. The center of gravity framework of Chapter 4 represents yet another view of how organizations grow and change over time, although it is more narrowly focused on issues of vertical integration and diversification.

THE POPULATION ECOLOGY VIEW

A uniform assumption that underlies both the growth and development models and the adaptation perspectives to be discussed in this chapter is that organizations adapt and change both their strategies and their organizational forms in the face of environmental threats. A distinctly different view, however, is offered by an emerging literature that employs a bioecologic analog in assessing organizational change, adaptation, and survival. This natural selection, or population ecology, framework argues that adaptation of organizational structures to environments occurs principally at the population level with forms of organization replacing each other as conditions change (Hannan and Freeman 1984).

Structural inertia is seen as the primary element that limits and slows organizational change. Both internal and external factors contribute to the inertia of an organization, including the existing asset, employee, and customer base of the firm; legal requirements; and other competitive entry/exit barriers. Accordingly, it is extremely difficult for firms to radically alter their strategy or structure.

Survival of some organizational forms (populations) can be seen as a process of natural selection, which begins with variations in existing forms, either purposeful or unintended. Some variations prove more beneficial than others in acquiring resources from the environment that contribute to the survival of that organizational form in the competitive struggle (McKelvey and Aldrich 1983). Beneficial variations will be retained by firms that have them and will be copied by competing firms. Based upon the preceding, those organizational forms that have a fit with the environment are "selected out" for survival.

Note that this view does not exclude the possibility of adaptation on the part of the firm, but rather argues that such adaptation is far less common than traditional management literatures suggest. This is largely due to the element of uncertainty. Even when firms attempt to act rationally, their actions can be interpreted as random as long as the link between actions and outcomes remains unclear due to environmental uncertainty. Interestingly, firms that have attained a strong fit between their structural form and the environment are characterized as gaining increased structural inertia. This helps to maintain a tight fit with the environment but also makes change and adaptation in the future less probable.

One clear contribution of this stream of literature is to move researchers toward the development of theories that are posited to obtain for like organizations. That is, the movement is away from theories supposedly pertinent to all organizations or thought to obtain to only a single firm. Although an intriguing perspective that bears observation for future development, the population ecology framework raises as many questions as it answers. For example, what constitutes a population of organizations? How does this view explain the number of studies (such as those included in this chapter) that describe numerous adaptations observed of both individual firms as well as industrial groupings of firms? Finally, what implications does this view have for decision making within individual firms?

MODELS OF ORGANIZATIONAL ADAPTATION

An underlying logic to the growth and development models to be discussed next builds upon Chandler's observation, consistent with economic theory, that changes on the part of the firm are a response to the need to employ resources more profitably, primarily due to changes in demand for the firm's products or services. Such demand changes are due to any number of environmental or industry structure factors.

However, the argument has been made that existing strategy and structure of the firm also influence strategic choices (Bower 1970). In contrast to the largely economic, rational view, Miles and Snow (1978) suggest that threats to the firm may be responded to in several ways. Building upon a more behavioral perspective, they argue that top decision makers are the primary link between the organization and its environment: "These top managers are viewed as being in a position not only to adjust organization structure and process when necessary but also to attempt to manipulate the environment itself in order to bring it into conformity with what the organization is already doing" (Miles and Snow 1978, 20).

In the process of change and adaptation, three primary problems are viewed as part of the adaptive cycle for all firms. The *entrepreneurial problem* centers on the development of innovations to strengthen the firm's competitive position. The *engineering problem* involves the creation of mechanisms that implement management's response to the entrepreneurial problem. The *administrative problem* centers on stabilizing and institutionalizing those solutions to the entrepreneurial and engineering problems while positioning the organization to continue to adapt to subsequent challenges. The three problems are highly interrelated, and many times firms may face them in the sequence as listed. Nonetheless, the cycle can be triggered at any one of the three points.

Based upon a review of the literature and their own empirical observations across several industries, Miles and Snow identified the following four archetypes of organizational adaptation. These adaptation types, or modes, are intended to capture a holistic view of the organization, its internal structure and process, and the nature of its interactions with its environment.

1. *Defenders* are organizations which have narrow product-market domains. Top managers in this type of organization are highly expert in their organization's limited area of operation but do not tend to search outside of their domains for new opportunities. As a result of this narrow focus, these organizations seldom need to

make major adjustments in their technology, structure, or methods of operation. Instead, they devote primary attention to improving the efficiency of their existing operations.

2. *Prospectors* are organizations which almost continually search for market opportunities, and they regularly experiment with potential responses to emerging environmental trends. Thus, these organizations often are the creators of change and uncertainty to which their competitors must respond. However, because of their strong concern for product and market innovation, these organizations usually are not completely efficient.

3. *Analyzers* are organizations which operate in two types of product-market domains, one relatively stable, the other changing. In their more turbulent areas, top managers watch their competitors closely for new ideas, and then they rapidly adopt those which appear to be the most promising.

4. *Reactors* are organizations in which top managers frequently perceive change and uncertainty occurring in their organizational environments but are unable to respond effectively. Because this type of organization lacks a consistent strategy-structure relationship, it seldom makes adjustments of any sort until forced to do so by environmental pressures. (Miles and Snow 1978, 29)

This framework and specific related hypotheses were tested by the authors in several different industrial settings: college textbook publishing, food processing, and hospitals.

Subsequently, Miles (1982) used the framework in their longitudinal study of the adaptation strategies employed by firms in the tobacco industry, which was threatened with declining domestic demand and increased government intervention. He found that the firms in this industry could well be categorized as defenders, prospectors, analyzers, and reactors. Additionally, however, he found that the strategic responses on the part of these firms fell into three categories:

- *Domain defense* directed at the restoration of the legitimacy of the traditional business;
- *Domain offense* centering on activities to maintain the individual firm's share of a stagnating market; and
- *Domain creation*, which was the movement into product-market areas new to the firm, primarily through product and geographic diversification.

These studies tend to reinforce the validity of the framework and to suggest that the perceptions and choices of the dominant coalition of managers strongly influence both the internal structure of the organization and how the organization positions itself in the environment. No one adaptive model is proposed as superior to others, as several have been employed successfully at the same time by different firms in the same environmental setting. However, each mode must be implemented with an appropriate configuration of internal structure and process.

Finally, an alternative typology of adaptation was developed by Miller and Friesen (1980a, 1980b) in the analysis of 135 transition periods gleaned from the published histories of thirty-six firms. Supported with additional questionnaire data, they extracted nine archetypes of organizational transition, which provide some feeling for how a firm adapts. However, in contrast to Miles and Snow and to the growth and development models to be discussed in the next section, the reference to strategy in this view is more general. Additionally, the Miller and Friesen types describe a specific transition that a firm could experience; indeed, the same firm could and probably does experience several of the types over its history. The Miller and Friesen types include adaptations beyond major strategy-structure realignments. Examples of the types that they identified include entrepreneurial revitalization, consolidation, movement toward stagnation, troubleshooting, and fragmentation.

GROWTH AND DEVELOPMENT MODELS

When a number of organizations repeat the same sequence of major structural changes, researchers propose that something systematic is at work and that different stages of organizational growth may be involved, with each stage having its own peculiar combination of structure, process, reward, and people dimensions. This section reviews the various models that have been proposed for different strategy-structure stages of growth and development.

Every area of inquiry has its own stages model. One can find proposed stages in individual cognitive development and socioemotional development, in group development, and in the economic development of countries. Organization and management theory is no exception. Several reviews of this literature already exist and are not repeated here (Starbuck 1965, 1971; Child and Keiser 1978). Instead, we have selected only those models that are relevant to choices of strategy and structure.

In a recent literature review, Kazanjian (1983) uncovered over twenty stage-developmental models of organizations, each with varying strategic and organizational elements included. Some models are postulated to obtain for all organizations, while others are theorized relevant for only certain types of firms. The stage of growth models of interest here grew out of the Chandler research and focus primarily on the firm's response to increased complexity associat~d with growth and diversification in its various forms. Ultimately, t.. following questions are investigated: What constitutes a stage in these developmental sequences? How many stages are there? Is the sequence unalterable? How does one distinguish one stage from another?

Scott's Three-Stage Model

Chandler's research has been summarized and extended by Scott (1971). His three-stage model, however, does not include all of Chandler's stages. Recall that Chandler proposed a sequence of changes that begins with the small enterprise. He suggested that the first strategy was simply an expansion of volume. The increase in output required separation of an administrative component that is distinct from the work-performing component. The next strategy was to increase volume by expanding geographically. The multiple geographic units posed new administrative problems with regard to headquarters–field unit relations. This problem is the classic centralization-decentralization issue. These two forms are grouped together to form Stage I in the Scott model. The result is a simple organization performing a single function, such as manufacturing, for a single product line. It provides a good starting point for the complexity models.

The first increase in complexity by American firms was initiated by a strategy of vertical integration. That is, the simple firm began to acquire other functions, such as the distribution and selling functions. By this means, diverse functions were added. These sequential functions posed new administrative problems in managing horizontal work flows, however. The result was the invention of the functional organization and of processes of forecasting and scheduling. These firms learned to manage multiple functions but remained within a single product line. This type of firm was Scott's Stage II form.

The next stage starts with the pursuit of a strategy of product diversification. The management of multiple product lines posed problems of measurement of relative financial performance and allocation of capital across product lines. These problems were resolved by the adoption of the multidivisional structure in which each division was a functional organization producing a single product or limited line of products. Each division operated as a profit center. This profit-divisionalized firm was Scott's Stage III model. Scott extends the changes in structure to include changes in rewards, control, and so on. This model has been the most popular and widely quoted of the development models.

The essence of the Chandler and Scott sequences is the successive addition of new sources of diversity, which results in more complexity. Starting with the simple firm, which is single product, single function, and single region, there are successive adoptions of multiple regions, then multiple functions, and finally multiple products as the firm becomes a Stage I, Stage II, and finally a Stage III organization. The change from stage to stage constitutes a metamorphosis.

Salter Model

The Scott model has been analyzed and extended by Salter (1970). He suggested that the Scott model misses two forms of organization and thereby also misses the possible alternative paths that can be taken through developmental sequences. For example, the multidivisional forms that were adopted by General Motors and Du Pont were achieved through different transitions. General Motors was a holding company, while Du Pont was a Stage II functional organization. The holding company form is not in the model. In addition, Salter proposes that the geographic multidivisional form should be a separate stage. Thus, he splits Scott's Stage III form into a Stage 3, the geographic form, and a Stage 4, the product form. However, he does not include the holding company as a separate form or stage.

The Salter work raises the question of what constitutes a stage. A multidivisional structure around geographic areas is different from a multidivisional structure around product lines. But is it different enough to constitute a separate stage? How different must it be? How does one tell? Our view is that the geographic profit center is not a separate stage. Although the transition from geographic to product divisionalized form or vice versa would require a major change in the power structure of an organization, it would not constitute a major change in the "way of life" in the organization. It is still a profit center or investment center of one dimension (i.e., product or region). The managerial style is still one of delegation of operations to the divisions, and the rewards are based on bottom-line results. The change is nowhere near the magnitude of that which occurs in the change from a functional form to a profit center form. Our contention is that characteristics of structure, process, reward, and people are quite similar for all multidivisional forms regardless of what the one dimension is. That is, the multidivisional structure can be based upon products, regions, markets, industries, and so on, and the way of life will be similar. That way of life will change only when other dimensions or sources of diversity are added, or when the geographic expansion is international rather than domestic.

Stopford Model

Another extension of the Scott model has been proposed by Stopford to account for the international expansion of American firms (Stopford 1968; Stopford and Wells 1972). According to his two-stage model of movement into international markets, the firms first formed an international division and attached it to their domestic product divisions. The division was then disbanded, and either worldwide product divisions or area divisions were adopted. Product divisions resulted from the high foreign product diversification, and area divisions were adopted for low product diversity. However, Stopford did not suggest that these structural forms constituted a new stage. Instead he called them Stage III with an international division and Stage III other, meaning that the form could be product, area, or even some mixture of the two. The question naturally arises whether these two types are Stages IV and V, representing a type genuinely different from Stage III domestic firms.

Our view is that the international division is not a new stage. The addition of a new geographic division—even an international division—has about the same impact as the addition of a new business or product division. The move to a global structure of either worldwide product divisions or area divisions poses a problem, however. On the one hand, the global structures are still unidimensional profit centers. On the other hand, the global structures are significant departures from the pure domestic multidivisional structure. In addition, there is no single global form. An organization can be a global divisional structure as already mentioned, a global holding company, or a global functional organization. We deal first with how the global structures differ from pure domestic form, then with differences among the multiple forms.

The difference between global and domestic multidivisionals is best illustrated by the phases through which the global structure is established. It takes place over an extended period of time and entails establishing an international operation that is integrated with domestic operations. Both operations are modified in the process of becoming a global company. The transition is best illustrated by the work of Smith and Charmoz (1975) in their analysis of American pharmaceutical companies that expanded internationally. Since their work was not presented earlier, it is reviewed briefly here.

Smith and Charmoz Model

Smith and Charmoz report that predictable problems arise in the growth of the multinational corporations, because the U.S. organization must invent coordination and control devices in the international sphere, since the existing devices were designed for domestic operations. They invented control mechanisms for domestic operations before going international; therefore they must start again with Stages I, II, and III on an international basis. The evolution is one of establishing control points that move from country to the corporate level, as the organization moves from the initial steps to a global enterprise. They propose a five-phase model for this evolution, which is illustrated in Figure 8.1.

Phase I represents the first move into a new area, an action that is guided by an attempt to minimize risk. The capital risk is minimized by using local distributors and participating in joint ventures. This allows the U.S. firm to learn the ropes. Often, returns on the original investments are held as reserves against future losses. During this phase, there are no systems to process international information, no international staffs, and no plans or strategies. Decisions are made through direct personal contract as problems arise. Control is located at the corporate office, because new operations need cash.

An overload at the top provokes a move to Phase II. Either too many decisions must be made, or not enough decisions are made. Whatever the case may be, the result is that the subsidiaries go their own way. Also, because of the lack of time and expertise at the top, poor decisions are often made.

Phase II is marked by subsidiary development and the appointment of an international executive staff. The executive acts to support the subsidiaries and allocates capital accordingly. Large subsidiaries therefore get the most attention because they require most of the investment. Control now moves into the hands of the subsidiaries, who initiate, propose, and act. The domestic company is essentially left out of the process because of its lack of knowledge. Up to this point, there has been little movement of people to the international division, and U.S.-centered thinking still predominates. Control remains on a basis of personal contact between the international executive and both corporate offices and subsidiaries. By the end of Phase II, however, the international executives become overwhelmed. They are continuously traveling and have little, if any, time left to plan. Subsidiary managers begin to run their subsidiaries according to their own needs, not the corporate office's. Competition between subsidiaries develops over new areas and territories.

Phase III, then, can be called the phase of regionalization. A

*Figure 8.1   Evolution of Control, Coordination,
and Organizational Crises in the Development of MNC*

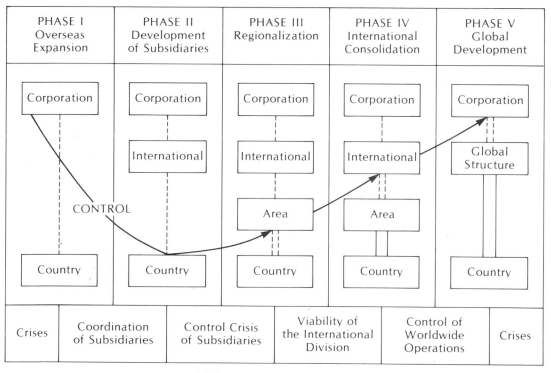

COORDINATION PATTERNS

- - - - Mutual Adjustment (Coordination by checking only as problems arise)

= = = = Planning (Coordination through top down planning)

_____ Policy and Procedure (Coordination through establishment of policies and procedures)

SOURCE: Smith and Charmoz (1975).

Source: Smith and Charmoz (1975).

regional international executive is added, as well as staffs, and possible rationalizations are made for cross-border moves. These moves require a regional plan. Impersonal planning control replaces personal contact as control moves from subsidiary to region. By now the corporation recognizes the international group as a source of investment and is no longer satisfied with informal personal decision making. Use of return on investment criteria either is instituted across the board or is modified for the differential risk levels of countries. The international president is now a politician, a buffer. Since little data are available for making decisions, the domestic executives are ignorant of the international affairs. The international president must simultaneously get support from domestic product divisions and ward off ignorant staff groups who want information, and may flood the fledgling subsidiaries with procedures.

The international president may be seen as a block by both international and domestic subsidiaries. At this point, the domestic subsidiaries and corporate offices realize how little they know about the international group and notice that the international group is a competitor for capital, research and development, people, and so forth. The problem at this point, however, is to prevent a move to a global structure that would be premature, because staffs are still ignorant about international affairs, and there are no planning and information systems to provide a link with the corporate office.

Phase IV is marked by international consolidation. In this stage, control moves to the international CEO to bring order and rationality to the dispersion characterizing the previous three periods of development. This period is one in which the corporate officers take a real and direct interest in the international divisions. The size of investments and interdependency of areas dictate a greater degree of centralization. However, there are not blanket solutions here, because of the differential rate of development of the geographic areas and the firm's own product lines. Most firms differ in the establishment of distinctive patterns of coordination. International consolidation is marked by executive international committees, planning and evaluation systems, more sophisticated financial measures, and task forces. By now the international division rivals the domestic divisions even more. The need is increasingly greater for worldwide data and for a global mechanism to overcome parochial local interests. The corporate staff wants more control and information at this point; the area managers resent the planning and control. The international executive may again moderate a still ignorant staff, since the corporate officers might press prematurely for the kind of "planning control" that is better suited for the next phase of development.

Phase V, which can be termed "global development," is marked by corporate control. Through the increased contacts of the previous phase, corporate and domestic product groups have a more realistic awareness of foreign operations. The "planning" coordination provided by the international division is now superfluous. The particular organizational format that evolves is governed by product diversity and proportion of foreign sales as presented by Stopford. Phase V is also marked by a significant improvement in global information and planning systems. Most companies maintain some form of international specialist coordination. This role is more integrative than controlling.

Our view is that transition to a global structure constitutes a metamorphosis. Changes occur in the financial control system designed to handle such factors as national variations, profits by product and region, and transfer pricing. Different and multiple standards of evaluation appear, careers and compensation practices are changed, and new committees and staffs evolve. Most important, an international mentality gets created to various degrees. All together, we believe these changes constitute a different way of life and therefore a different form.

The global form is not, however, a single distinct form like a functional or holding company form. There is no single global form. In its different manifestations it resembles the multidivisional forms that are all profit centers but in which the profit center could be based on products, markets, or regions. Global structures can also assume any of those three multidivisional forms, or they can take a global functional or a holding company form. Thus, we conceive of four different types of organization, each of which constitutes a distinct way of life: the simple, the functional, the holding company (or conglomerate), and the multidivisional form. Each of these types can (but probably only the latter three do) exist in a domestic or in a global form. We prefer to talk about these eight possible organizations as forms rather than as stages. All the forms are possible. Whether there are stages is in part an empirical question. Two studies have addressed this question.

Stopford and Franko Studies

Two major empirical studies have dealt with the stage of growth of American multinationals and European multinationals, respectively. Both offer findings concerning the sequence of the stages.

According to Stopford and Wells (1972), the American multinational's first phase in international growth is characterized by an initial period of autonomy for the foreign subsidiary. The second phase is a period of organizational consolidation when an international division is developed. The international division is typically considered an independent enterprise and is not subject to the same strategic planning that guides domestic activities. In the third phase, strategic planning is carried out on a consistent and worldwide basis, and the structure of the foreign activities is altered to provide closer links with the rest of the structure. This research indicates that most American firms went through one of two major sequences of structural change.

The firms either moved from a functional Stage II structure to a divisional Stage III structure for their domestic businesses before adding an international division, or added an international division to a domestic Stage III structure. Stopford and Wells found that forty-nine of fifty-seven firms that replaced their international divisions did so after they had developed Stage III structures for their domestic activities. The few firms that moved directly from a Stage II structure with an international division to a global system are exceptions to the trend, and all of them adopted area divisions.

Unlike American multinationals, European enterprises that adopted supranational organizational structures typically did so after achieving a relatively large spread of multinational operations (Franko 1974, 1976). Moreover, when the continental multinationals changed their organizational structure, they also did so in a sequence very different from that followed by their American counterparts.

One sees that most continental firms simply skipped the international division phase passed through by nearly 90 percent of the American multinationals surveyed. One also observes that in all but three cases, continental moves to the global forms of worldwide product divisions, area divisions, or mixed and matrix structures accompanied rather than followed divisionalization moves at home. In contrast, more than three-quarters of the American enterprises classified as multinational saw fit to change their domestic organizational structures from functional to divisional prior to adopting one of the so-called global structures.

In the competitive environment of their home market, American firms adapted their structures to their product diversification strategies. In practice, this meant that diversified American firms forsook functional for divisional organizational structures well before they had had much of a chance to involve themselves in foreign operations.

Further examination of the data reveals some consistency between the European and American experiences. Those firms that did establish international divisions were French and German firms that came from large countries with large domestic markets. Also, if Europe is considered a single market, then many firms manage the rest of the world through an international division. Both these observations lend support to the international division stage, provided that there is a large domestic market.

In summary, these studies support the stagewise thesis of growth from a domestic functional organization to global multidivisional structures. They also repeat Salter's assertion of alternate paths to worldwide structures. As organizations come from different size countries, face domestic markets varying in competitiveness, and grow by acquisition rather than internally, they choose different but predictable paths to a similar final stage. However, the more detailed the specification of the stage, the less predictable the sequential movement. As long as we conceive of only three stages, with global forms considered to be a Stage III type, the stages of growth model holds. As soon as we consider other types of global structure or consider substages such as the international division phase, more alternate paths appear, more outcomes are possible, and more detailed specifications of strategy, such as Rumelt's nine categories, are required to match strategy with structure and process.

A Revised Model

In this section, we offer our model of growth and development, which summarizes the thinking of others and builds on the empirical evidence. The model is based upon several assumptions and empirical findings. The first assumption is that starting with the simple form, any source of diversity could be added to move to a new form. There is no set sequence through which firms must move in lockstep. An organization could add functions, products, and geography and wind up with a global multidivisional form or by passing instead through functional and global functional forms as intermediate transitions. As a result of this assumption, alternate paths through the developmental sequence are possible. The comparison of American and European multinationals is a case in point.

Although alternative paths are possible, a dominant sequence emerges empirically. Both Franko and Stopford report dominant sequences when multiple sequences are possible. This result is attributable in part to the effects of the environment. When faced with similar environments, firms choose to do similar things. The particular scenario that emerged consisted of specific patterns of population growth, economic growth, technological change, and political changes. Particular strategies resulting in particular structures proved to be profitable at various times. However, if a different scenario could have emerged, then a different dominant sequence would be observed. The point is that there is no set sequence; in all cases, however, development was dominated by the particular pattern of organizational growth. Even though a pattern dominates, other routes are taken by a minority of the firms.

Another feature of all developmental models is that an organization can stop anywhere along the way. Not every American organization is going to become a global multidivisional firm. Various niches can be found, and any of the forms can be adopted that happen to fit that niche. Also, a firm can reverse direction and retrace its steps. Some firms are busy selling off their international subsidiaries and could very well move back to a domestic multidivisional.

Finally, the resulting structure of any sequence of development is, as Chandler suggested, a concatenation of all previous steps. If one examined global structure based on areas, one would find that within an area, structure is based on products. Within the product substructure, the organization could be market based by breaking out government and commercial sectors. Within a market sector, the substructure is probably functional. Thus, each level of the hierarchy is a mechanism for coping with a source of diversity.

The resulting stages model is shown in Figure 8.2. The starting point is the simple structure with one function and product line. The first major structural change results from a growth in volume. The increased size brings about a division of labor and the simple functional organization to coordinate the divided work. From this structure several paths are possible. Some firms with crucial supply or distribution problems will pursue strategies of vertical integration. These forms will continue to elaborate the functional organization into large, centralized firms. The mining companies are good examples. Other organizations will diversify product lines through internal growth and acquisition. The internal developer tending to pursue a related diversification strategy will adopt the multidivisional structure. The third path an organization can follow is to diversify through acquisition and pursue an unrelated diversification strategy. These firms would adopt a holding company or conglomerate form. In each case, the structure fits the strategy.

Although the next stages increase rapidly in number of possibilities, empirically there is a dominant movement. The majority of large enterprises have moved to the multidivisional form either from a holding company type like General Motors or from a functional form as did Du Pont. In the former case, the move is an attempt to consolidate acquisitions, exploit a source of relatedness, and switch to internal growth. The latter case in the classic example of a functional organization unable to manage diversity.

Two other possible paths are not observed in the particular sample of firms that make up the empirical studies reviewed. The multidivisional could change to the centralized functional form or to the holding company model. A firm could introduce standardization across related product lines and attempt to exploit economies of scale by moving to the functional organization. General Motors may be an example. In its automobile business, General Motors had moved toward a more functional organization by placing all manufacturing in a GM Assembly Division. More recently, it has moved toward more centralization of engineering, operations, and other nonmarketing tasks with the creation of its large (Buick-Olds-

Figure 8.2   A Summary of Stages Model

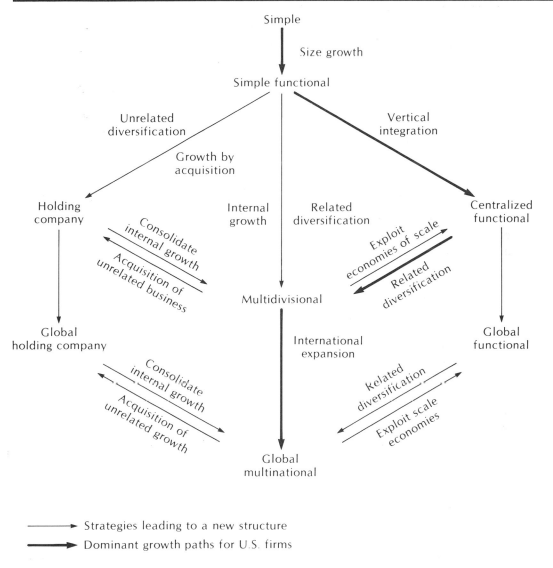

Cadillac) and small (Chevrolet-Pontiac-Canada) car groups. The creation of the new Saturn Division as a stand-alone group is in part a function of its nonstandard character in relation to existing product lines.

Alternatively, the multidivisional firm could pursue external growth and diversify into less-related businesses. A transition to a holding company could occur if the new acquisitions are not integrated into the existing structure. The original core business will probably become an autonomous group managed from its original location. Organizations not on the Fortune 500 have probably followed these paths.

The next different stage of development for those organizations that choose to pursue strategies of international expansion is the global form. Most organizations will adopt either the area or the product global form, as indicated in the Stopford research. Global holding companies and global functional forms are possible, too, although less likely.

In summary, firms do follow developmental sequences characterized by a metamorphosis between the stages. Also, a dominant path has been followed by large American enterprises. However, alternative paths are possible. We believe that referring to types of organizational form rather than to stages is preferable. The multidivisional form need not be Stage III. It can be Stage II for some firms who adopt a holding company for Stage III. Thus, the model proposed here allows alternative paths, permitting organizations to stop at any type and even to reverse direction. The primary point of the discussion is to separate what has been observed in a sample based study from what is possible.

A second feature of the model is that it does identify some stages of development. Not all paths are possible. An organization cannot move to a global form with passing through a domestic type as well. A simple organization cannot become a global multidivisional without passing through at least one transitional form. That is, an organization must learn to manage one to two sources of diversity before handling a third. In this sense, we can speak of stages, but we cannot equate any of the types of structure, after the simple structure, with a particular stage.

SUMMARY AND MANAGERIAL IMPLICATIONS

Three distinct perspectives of strategic adaptation have been reviewed in this chapter. First, the population ecology model proposes that populations of organizations with appropriate forms are selected by the environment for survival. Then, several frameworks, or typologies, of adaptive modes were reviewed, which suggest that preferences or skills of top managers will lead firms to respond to external challenges in a particular manner. The Miles and Snow typology of firms as defenders, prospectors, analyzers, and reactors is one example. Finally, a number of growth models have been reviewed.

Each of the growth models presents a sequence of stages through which all organizations must pass. The models differ in the number of stages but are similar in other respects. They see the change from one stage to another as a metamorphosis leading to a qualitatively different organization in that each stage consists of a package of structures, processes, systems, rewards, managerial styles, and so on. A movement to a new stage then requires a repackaging of all dimensions. Finally, a revised model employing types rather than stages was developed and presented.

The discussion of development and adaptation as well as that regarding the role of structure in earlier chapters now allows for a comprehensive explication of the strategy-structure relation.

The thesis that structure follows strategy has received substantial support. Large American and European manufacturing and service enterprises are diversifying products and markets. When they do, they adopt the multidivisional structure. The relation is shown in numerous studies. Clearly, something is at work here, but whether the relation is the one suggested by Chandler is not clear. The research has created other interpretations and additional variables that moderate the strategy-structure relation. We will follow the Scott and Chandler stages model here. No loss of general applicability is incurred as a result of substituting type for stage.

Chandler suggested that the Stage I structure was invented to solve the problems of the Stage I strategy (volume expansion). The Stage II structure was invented when Stage I structures could not manage the Stage II strategies, and so on. Thus, effective performance is achieved only when Stage N strategy is matched with Stage N structure. When management adopts an N + 1 strategy, a decline in performance occurs that provokes the shift to the N + 1 structure, which then increases performance. This sequence depicts the events at Du Pont that were described by Chandler. The observed lags in changes to multidivisional forms following diversification also fit the interpretation. Thus, a mismatch in strategy and structure causes a decline in performance that is restored when a match is finally achieved.

The direct tests of this hypothesis have not been conclusive and are subject to alternative explanations. Rumelt ran into difficulty because he could not always find mismatches in sufficient numbers to permit statistical tests. This fact could be taken as data that natural selection is at work, forcing mismatches into matches, but it may also be attributed to other factors, such as imitation of other organizations. In addition, the mismatches, although few in number, are sometimes the high performers. This observation is usually explained by the firm's having a temporary monopoly due to a hot, new product. When combined with the European research, these observations lead to the introduction of competition as a moderating variable in the strategy-structure relation.

The proposition becomes: *Only under competitive conditions does a mismatch between strategy and structure lead to ineffective performance.* If a firm has power over its environment so that it can control prices because of monopoly position, tariffs, or close ties to government, it can maintain effective economic performance even if a mismatch exists between strategy and structure. It does not have to engage in the difficult task of restructuring to bring about efficient internal resource allocations.

A couple of scenarios for firms under noncompetitive conditions are possible to augment the scenario put forth by Chandler and illustrated by the Du Pont case. One is that the adoption of an N + 1 strategy does not lead to a decline in performance at all. Thus, no motive exists for structural change. Second, a decline in performance may occur that is restored not by restructuring but by influencing relevant actors in the environment. Thus, the relation is not always a simple sequential process of change of strategy, decline in performance, restructuring, and restoration of performance. The relation becomes instead a complicated interplay between strategy, structure, performance, and competitiveness of markets.

The second scenario raises another possible sequence of events. Under competitive conditions, an N + 1 strategy and a Stage N structure will lead to a decline in performance. The interesting question is, What is the response of the organization to the information about performance? Presumably, performance can be restored either through restructuring or by influencing relevant actors in the environment. A third alternative is to return to the Stage *N* strategy and abandon the unfamiliar Stage N + 1. Conceivably, this third alternative may also restore performance.

The three possible scenarios, which could follow from a performance decline due to a mismatch, introduce another relavant variable: the power distribution among the top managers. Undoubtedly, proponents for all three alternatives can be found inside the firm. The functional vice-presidents will favor a return to the dominant business, whereas the younger managers with cross-functional experience may favor reorganization to the multidivisional form. Both positions are self-serving. In the absence of a clear-cut solution, the chosen alternative is the result of political processes. The greater the ambiguity, the greater the influence of politics in determining the outcome, and the greater the influence of the current distribution of power. Thus, structure will influence strategy. Also for this reason, a change in the chief executive is often needed to bring about the change in strategy and structure. The current organization has institutionalized the previous strategy, and role occupants stand to lose status and power by adopting a new strategy and, therefore, a new structure.

Therefore, the complete explanation of the relation between strategy and structure must consider a number of other factors. Figure 8.3 introduces these factors and illustrated some likely scenarios that can follow each condition. An adequate understanding requires knowledge of market conditions, performance, and the relative

Figure 8.3   *Schematic of Possible Strategy, Structure, and Performance Relations*

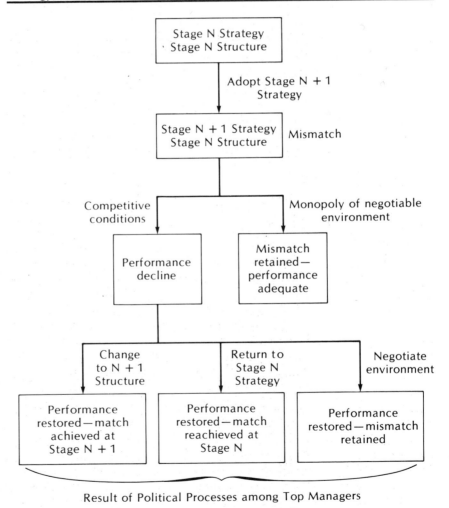

power of the dominant managers. A historical perspective upon the individual firm is required to untangle the interplay of these various factors.

Figure 8.3 and the prior discussion raise the issue of influence of structure upon strategy formulation. In the developmental sequence of Strategy I → Structure I → Strategy II → Structure II → Strategy III → Structure III, Chandler focused upon every other arrow. One could just as easily have focused upon the relation between Stage N structure and Stage N + 1 strategy. Strategy can also follow structure. Perhaps structure or organization can explain why some Stage II organizations adopted Stage III strategies and some did not. If Stage II strategy is matched with Stage II structure, why change? Chandler suggests that changes are a response to the need to employ resources more profitably because of shifts and growth in population, changes in technology, and so on.

Overall, then, consistency must exist between strategy and all elements of the structure. What is important is not whether structure causes strategy, or vice versa, but whether they are eventually brought into line. In many causal sequences, change of strategy may precede change of structure. Or performance may decline, precipitating first a strategy change and then a structure change. Or structure may be changed first to bring in new managers who will formulate the new strategy. There is no simple one-to-one relation such as structure follows strategy.

Our position is, It doesn't matter what you do, just as long as you do it well. That is, any situation has multiple solutions. What is important is choosing one of those solutions and pursuing it. The firm should match its structure to its strategy, match all components of the organization with one another, and match the strategy with the environment. The challenge is to understand, to learn how to manage, and to learn how to talk about the power dynamics that take place in the determination of the chosen strategy and structure. When stakes are high, when dedicated people win and lose, and when some people are hurt, these choices are crucial. The choices require greater understanding from theoretical, practical, and ethical perspectives.

9

Strategy and Organization: State of the Art

This last chapter discusses our view of the state of the art of the relation of strategy to organization. As has been the case historically, organizational or administrative advances emerge in response to new problems or managerial challenges. Based upon our present interaction with companies and our knowledge of their individual agendas of critical issues, three primary challenges, among others, will apparently be the focus of management attention and action across firms well into the next decade. The first of these challenges centers on the management of increased diversity, associated with the continuing trend toward diversification of products and markets. Second is the increasing globalization of markets and competition across industries. Finally, as a result of increased competition, there is the drive for innovation directed at product offerings, production processes, and administrative practices. Obviously, relationships between and among these three challenges can be established. However, each independently has implications for the strategic posture and choices of firms. Correspondingly, each challenge and the associated strategic choices will require a distinct configuration of organizational elements. This final chapter is structured around these three challenges and the associated strategic and organizational issues.

MANAGING DIVERSITY

As documented in earlier chapters, a continuing trend is toward diversification across all firms (not simply those that are U.S. based), which in some instances can add new sources of diversity—

for example, around markets or technologies—to the more standard sources of diversity: products or geography. Further, some firms have devised strategies that require equal priority to be given to two or more of such souces of diversity.

The result is an increase in interdependence between product divisions, business groups, area divisions, or whatever labels are used to name units. It is becoming virtually impossible to find clean, self-contained clusters of divisions or groups that can form profit centers. For example, the firms in the computer and communications industries must cope with the coordination of multiple functions when producing multiple products, whose technology is changing rapidly, for multiple countries and for multiple industries. Thus, one finds product managers, industry managers, functional managers, and area managers who focus upon each source of diversity. But multiple sources of diversity are not the only problem. The difficulty arises when product, geography, and market are of equal strategic importance. In the past, firms could manage diversity by choosing to organize differently at each level of the hierarchy. For example, in Figure 9.1, the electronics firm chose geography as the primary differentiating factor. Secondary emphasis is given to markets in an attempt to differentiate products going to consumers from products going to manufacturers. The next level differentiated between products. The product division was the basic profit center and was to coordinate the multiple functions, which were given fourth priority. The multiple sources of diversity were managed by the creation of multiple layers of management, each responsible for one of the sources. The level reflected the strategic priority.

The problem now is that geography and product are of equal priority, with technology so important that a single large research and development function is needed. All areas should sell the same minicomputer system rather than duplicate the development effort to create their own. Also, the minicomputer system needs to be compatible with the large-scale computing system so that they can be arranged to handle electronic funds transfer for the banking industry. The result is that some functions cannot be relegated to a fourth-level priority. Geography is important, but so are industry and product orientations. A great deal more interdependence exists across products, industries, areas, and functions. Self-contained profit centers are impossible to find, because a great deal of interunit coordination needs to take place. There is a need for more general management to provide the coordination. This is a critical administrative problem for the heavily diversified firm. How do you divide general management work so as to coordinate multiple sources of diversity, giving each equal priority? Many companies are grappling with this problem and creating new processes for managing it.

Figure 9.1   Standard Divisionalized Firm Emphasizing Geography

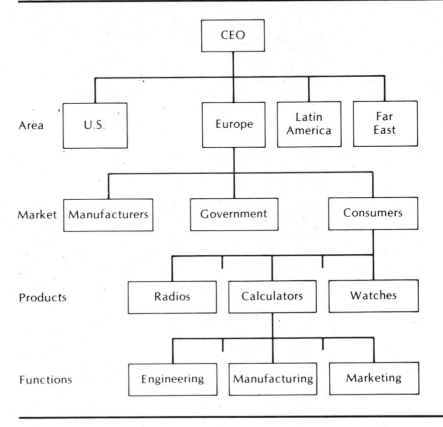

New Organizational Approaches to the Management of Diversity

The new strategies, which have increased the number and kinds of diversity and have assigned equal priority to two or more of them, have been implemented by many of the multinational organizations. They have evolved several new structures for dividing the additional general management work that is needed when several sources of diversity must be handled sumultaneously at the same level. Several of these solutions are variations on the Stage II hierarchical model discussed in earlier chapters. Others are matrix forms. The hierachical forms are discussed first.

Office of the Chief Executive.   One solution to the general management problem is to add one or more general managers who create an "office of the chief executive." The number varies from two to five, and division of responsibilities varies with the particular cast of characters. Some may be primarily concerned with external matters, others internal; or one may be concerned with international matters and one domestic. However, the key is that they think in terms of the corporation as a whole. Their performance is evaluated and their bonuses based on total corporate performance.

This form is chosen when no single piece of work can be broken off and set up as a self-contained group. For example, international activity may be spread throughout all the groups and cannot be separated from domestic activity. An additional general manager can be added to be primarily but not exclusively responsible for international activities and their linkage with domestic ones. The general manager would chair the world product line boards in addition to representing the corporation in the executive committee, on the board, and so on. Thus, when the need for coordination is scattered throughout the organization, the additional management can be added at the top to see that the integration is in the best interests of the organization as a whole. There is also a need for a cast of managers who can work as a team.

New General Management Positions. More recently, the logic of the idea behind the office of the chief executive has been extended to create new positions to manage critical functional interdependencies. For example, some technology-intense organizations have created the position of chief technical officer, who is responsible for coordinating and overseeing all technology-related matters across the firm, typically emphasizing the linkages between R&D and engineering. Both Gould and Activision have such a position, and Exxon has all central research and engineering under one executive. More as a span of control reducer for the CEO, some firms have moved to pull all central staff groups under a single administrative officer of the firm, such as a senior vice-president—administration. This off-loads the CEO to focus on line management and strategic matters.

New Self-Contained Clusters. Some organizations are able to add managers and create a layer between the chief executive and the group managers. These organizations are able to find a cluster of groups whose work is interdependent among themselves and relatively independent of other groups. For example, in the late 1970s, GE added a sector manager who managed all groups doing business in the consumer sector of the economy, as opposed to selling to industry or government. GE already had a four-person executive office and then had four levels of general management below it. The key for this choice is to be able to create a self-contained cluster of groups. In many instances, however, this option is not viable.

Group Executives with Two Hats.   An option that partially moves the organization toward a matrix form is to have group executives assume responsibility for two sources of diversity and, thereby, to wear two hats. For example, a geographically organized company had three major products that were sold across the geographic groups. To get economies of scale in product development, they wanted coordination across the groups. They felt they needed more than worldwide product boards. However, they also felt they did not need full-time product managers. As a result, three of the group managers were given a product responsibility in addition to the previous area responsibility.

The two-hat model is a partial matrix, because product managers in other areas report on a dotted line to an area group manager who has worldwide responsibility. It becomes important to manage the group executives as a team so that the inevitable conflicts can be raised in circumstances where they can be resolved with all geographic and product managers represented. Bonuses are usually paid on total profits, rather than on a product or geographic basis, to prevent biasing or suboptimization at corporate expense. To operate effectively, the solution requires new processes and rewards.

The two-hat model divides corporate office work among the group executives. It creates an active management committee instead of a new manager in the corporate office. In this model, group executives may spend up to half their time acting as part of the corporate office. This solution narrows the span of control of the group executive. Additional management must be added either immediately below the group executive or in the form of a new group executive. This particular form is popular among European firms. Royal Dutch Shell managers have both a functional and an area responsibility.

Matrix or Grid Forms.   The next alternative is to create a separate role for each source of diversity at the same level. This form was described in Chapter 7 for Dow-Corning, which has functional, business, and geographical managers all reporting to the office of the chief executive. Each source of diversity has its own champion, and the planning process is the resolver of conflict. Here, general management work is divided into pieces, with all pieces represented at the same level of the hierarchy. Work is sufficient for business managerial roles to be used, and businesses have equal priority with functions and areas. Care should be taken to recall all the processes, systems, and rewards that also accompany this structure.

New Planning Organizations—Strategic Business Units. The last response to diversity that is discussed here is the use of planning processes and a planning organization, which is different from the organization for execution. Many of these systems are labeled strategic business units (after the GE designation). Essentially, these processes are program, planning, and budgeting systems (PPBS) applied to business firms.

A study by Allen (1976) shows that the adoption of sophisticated planning, reward, and evaluation systems were the latest organizational innovations being created and adopted by American enterprise. Using a sample of forty American corporations, Allen followed changes in structure and process from 1970 to 1974. He found little change in structure but extensive changes in processes and systems. Many of these changes are probably attributable to the adoption of some form of the strategic business unit (SBU) structure.

More recently, a majority of the firms have chosen to use the office concept and the sector level. Many tried matrix and planning systems, but most retreated from them. No studies report exact numbers for matrix, but experience and a familiarity with the business press lead one to that conclusion. One study does report that 7 percent of the firms in their sample had planning structures different from the organizational structures to implement the plan (Davidson and Haspeslagh 1982). But in the international arena, matrix and newer structures are evolving.

Is Matrix the New Stage Organizational Form?

Much of the research cited in Chapters 2, 3, and 8 has been based on the precise stagewise development of organizations as originally described by Chandler. Most of those authors, however, beg the question as to whether we are entering a new stage. Stopford and Wells (1972) extended Scott's Stage III organization into Stage III with an international division and Stage III global structures, which we call the G-form. The question now becomes, How much further can the Stage III type be extended before it becomes another type? The question is specifically suggested in Stopford's diagram, which is reproduced in Figure 9.2.

What happens to worldwide product divisions as volume increases? Can they take a united stance to adapt to the European community or to local host government demands? What happens to area divisions when they diversify and upgrade technology? The question marks in Figure 9.2 symbolize these questions.

In the previous edition of this work, we stated that some research that appeared in the late seventies suggested that matrix organiza-

Figure 9.2   Stage IV Conditions

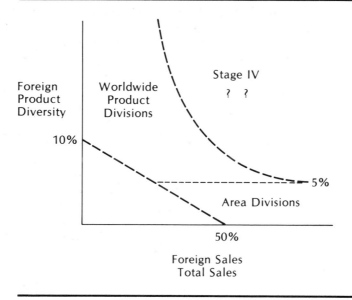

tion was becoming the Stage IV organization (Allen 1973, 1978; Lawrence and Davis 1978; Miles and Snow 1978). The opinions of these authors assert that the question marks are being replaced by grid and matrix structures, and that matrix, grid, or simultaneous structures are indeed a new type of structure. Why? Because they represent a genuinely different way of life. We have always had multiple influence channels in line and staff organizations, but the matrix is an organization with two (or more) line structures, two accounting systems, two bases of rewards, two budgeting systems, and so forth. When the unity of command principle or the single tie-breaker role disappears, the way of life changes. Lawrence and Davis describe the change as not simply a change to a matrix structure, but rather as the creation of matrix systems (budget information, rewards, performance appraisal, careers, and so on), the generation of matrix behavior, and finally, the institutionalization of a matrix culture. The matrix culture is lasting, because as we have argued, structure, systems, and processes must change as strategies and environments change. This matrix culture is essentially a conflict resolution system through which resources get allocated in the face of diverse demands for them.

In recent years, however, matrix organization has received considerable bad publicity. Some organizations have announced that they have experienced operating problems because of an overly complicated matrix structure. Still others have announced that they have gone away from matrix. Perhaps the most telling blow was the assertion in *In Search of Excellence* that none of the excellent companies used a matrix organization (Peters and Waterman 1982). In many business circles, the word is out that "matrix doesn't work."

Our response to those espousing this view is that they are partly correct and partly not. They are partly correct in that matrix organization did not fulfill its promise at many companies and was harmful to some. The reasons for the poor performance are varied. Some companies adopted matrix because it was fashionable. Along with SBUs, quality circles, and growth-share matrices, a self-respecting executive needed a matrix organization to round out the repertoire. In many cases, matrix did not fit the business situation, caused operating problems, and was abandoned by saying, "Matrix doesn't work."

Matrix was abandoned at other companies, however, even though it did fit the business. Two main reasons accounted for these failures. First, matrix was often inappropriately implemented. Matrix is an inherently collaborative and participative structure. It was often unilaterally announced and imposed through the hierarchy and then abandoned when the troops resisted the imposition and the obvious contradiction.

In other cases, implementation failures were more subtle. Companies tried to implement matrix while pursuing a strategy for which matrix was appropriate, but also failed to obtain the expected results as they pressed their organizations beyond their capacity for change. In these circumstances, the gap between the old structure and the new matrix organization was too large to be overcome in the time period in question. For example, some Bell System companies tried matrix when business segments were introduced. In multiregion companies, the multiple businesses were organized as a matrix across the previous geographic profit centers. Many of these companies experienced difficulty despite the appropriateness of matrix. These companies remained conscious of hierarchical levels, had no performance measurements, budgets, or planning processes for businesses, perpetuated a tradition of internal competition which should have been converted to cooperation, and so on. The transition problem to create a whole new organization was enormous. The promise of matrix was never attained.

The second reason related to the abandonment of matrix was strategic. For some firms, business conditions changed. In the electronics industry, for example, the time-to-market for new products decreased dramatically as product life cycles collapsed down to three to five years. New, small start-up companies were able to react quickly to these shortened lead times. In response, large organizations then converted from matrix to small, self-contained divisions to focus on rapid new product development. In this situation, matrix and its resource-sharing capabilities should be abandoned for faster-responding, less-efficient divisions. In neither of these cases, however, can it be said that matrix per se doesn't work.

In all of the prior cases, the results attained under matrix were poor. The managements and observers of these firms then concluded that matrix doesn't work. However, in no case is the problem matrix per se. Matrix continues to be the only organizational form that fits the strategy of simultaneous pursuit of multiple business dimensions, with each given equal priority. Admittedly, matrix is a very demanding organization. The managements are put to the task of learning new structures, new processes, new planning systems, new performance measures, new reward systems, and so on. But the response of today's managers to matrix is almost identical to the response of managers earlier in this century to the multidivisional form as described in Chandler. The stories of General Motors and Du Pont describe mistakes, false starts, resistance, and abandonment of early attempts at new structures. Eventually, the structural form succeeds because it fits the situation. Thus, matrix can work when it evolves, not when it is installed.

Overall, our view is that many failures have been associated with matrix organization. However, we believe that the failures are not because "matrix doesn't work" but because managements have failed at implementing matrix. On some other occasions, matrix was abandoned because the situation changed. Matrix was abandoned in the same way that functional organizations were abandoned for divisional profit centers. Functional and matrix organizations both work, but only for particular strategic problems.

The assertion that matrix can work is also based on the fact that some companies have been successful with it. Here, our experience is exactly opposite to that of the authors of *In Search of Excellence*. It is among the excellent companies that one would expect to find the difficult forms of management such as matrix being implemented successfully. Intel, Motorola, IBM, Procter and Gamble, Digital, and Boeing are all excellent companies with whom we have worked and who use matrix management. They may or may not use the term *matrix* to describe their own organization, however. Also, if we focus on the international portion of the business, the use of matrix and matrixlike structures has increased. In terms of new products introduced and growth in sales, the matrix outperforms the worldwide product division structure (Davidson and Haspeslagh 1982). Thus, we still believe matrix to be a Stage IV organization. Further, we argue that it is an essential form for the conduct of diversified, multinational enterprises that aspire to be effective international competitors. We now turn to issues related to the management of the global firm—the second strategic challenge.

MANAGING TO THE GLOBAL CHALLENGE

The challenge of competing on a global basis, beyond issues regarding the management of diversity described previously, is causing firms to fashion new strategies and therefore new organizations (Hamel and Prahalad 1985). A primary source of the challenge comes from the Japanese (Kotler, Fahey, and Jatusripitak 1985). Let us briefly review the international development of American companies and then present the new challenges brought on by the Japanese and global competition.

In Chapter 3, we presented the results of the international strategy and structure studies. Figure 9.3 presents these results and the extensions to the new challenges to be discussed here. The area divisions and the worldwide product divisions have both come under pressure because of the multidimensional issues described earlier in the chapter.

Problems with Geographic or Area Divisions

The area divisions or groups, and country profit centers of multinational firms have three primary issues with which to deal. The first is the homogenizing of markets and the design of universal products for them. Geographic differences in markets and local adaptation of products led to countries or regions being the basic profit centers. As local differences decline, the need for local adaptation declines, and with it the need for local geographic profit centers. The effect of homogenizing markets gets amplified when combined with the other two issues. One is drive for economies of scale and the increasing use of world-scale plants. Every country cannot afford its own manufacturing facilities. In semiconductors, the next plant now costs over $100 million. With the universal products being produced in world-scale plants, the decision making moves out of countries and regions and to the worldwide headquarters. The third issue, the most powerful reducer of country autonomy, is the development of technology. As the investment in R&D becomes substantial, individual countries cannot stay in the game, as technology development evidences clear economies of scope. In addition, technology does not change at country boundaries. The third law of thermodynamics is the same in every country of the world. When the universality of

Figure 9.3   *International Strategy and Organization*

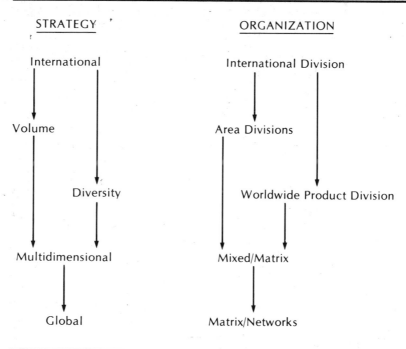

technology is combined with the homogenization of markets and need for world-scale plants, geography becomes a less important basis for thinking about a business and for organizing profit centers. Thus, worldwide product organizations would apparently be ideally designed for the new technical realities.

Problems with Worldwide Product Divisions

The worldwide product form of organization would have been the clear alternative means of organizing if it had not developed some problems of its own. The first is the relationship with more active host governments. Local governments do not sit idly by as manufacturing and technology development shift to other countries, and then import those products. They have shifted from using tariffs and quotas to industrial policies requiring local content, export, and local technology development. These policies require a relationship and negotiations with local government. This relationship is best handled by local country managers and geographic organizations. If the negotiations are not fruitful, then many advantages of worldwide products and sourcing are not attained.

The organizations using the worldwide product structures have also underperformed in international markets. The product form was to lead to better use of new technology, newer products, and better transfer to international markets. They have not performed as well as companies with international divisions or matrix organizations (Davidson and Haspeslagh 1982). Instead of introducing new products overseas, the product organizations used licenses and reduced direct investment. The product divisions tended to be dominated by domestic management who saw international investments as more risky. Riskier still, in the eyes of domestic-oriented managers, were investments in new countries in which the company is not now doing business. Product-organized companies seemingly are poor at breaking into new geographic markets.

Multidimensional Strategies

The effects of the economies necessary for manufacturing and technology development, and the need for responsiveness to local governments lead companies to view their strategies as multidimensional ones, much as was described at the beginning of this chapter. These companies must simultaneously emphasize geography and businesses.

The organizational result has been a move to matrixlike structures and mixed structures. For example, organizations that pursued area structures kept these geographic profit centers but added worldwide product managers. Colgate-Palmolive has always had strong country managers. But as they doubled the funding for product research, and as Colgate Dental Creme became a universal product, product managers were added at corporate to direct the R&D funding and coordinate marketing programs worldwide.

Similarly, the product-divisionalized firms have been reintroducing the international division. At Motorola, the product groups had worldwide responsibility for their product lines. As they compete with the Japanese in Japan, an international group has been introduced to help coordinate across product lines in Japan.

The added organizational units vary in their strengths. Some are full matrix organizations, while others utilize integrating roles as described in Chapter 5. Other organizations are using mixed structures. One company runs its pharmaceutical group as a worldwide entity. Pharmaceutical companies invest 15 to 20 percent of sales back into R&D. The products are the same in each country to meet medical claims made to ministries of health. The company's health, beauty care, and toiletries product lines are managed in a matrix of product lines across countries. The new countries in the Far East are managed as stand-alone country profit centers. Thus, the company mixes worldwide product, country, and matrix structures as the need dictates.

Global Strategies

New challenges are already appearing, requiring global strategies. These challenges come from global competitors and global customers who act on a global basis. In addition, the economies of scale for manufacturing and technology, and active local governments are increasing their respective effects on strategy and organization. Not all companies are experiencing these global challenges, but others are deep into these issues.

Global competitors have been around for some time. However, only in the past few years has the impact of global competition been felt across many industries and the issue given a high priority. The Japanese, in particular, think and act on a global basis. They will launch an attack on a competitor in a particular market by cutting price. They will subsidize the losses in that country market with profits from another country market where the competitor cannot respond. The firm being targeted is usually a high-share domestic company. The only response for the target company is to cut costs and prices and ask for protection. The entire battle gets fought in the targeted company's market. Some 70 to 80 percent of its revenue base comes under margin pressure. The attacking company, with 5 percent of its revenue under margin pressure, is willing to sustain the fight. The only effective response is for the target company to attack the attacker in its profit sanctuary, thereby putting a large portion of revenue under margin pressure (Watson 1982).

The global competitor is one who cross-subsidizes countries in the fight for market share. The new game in global competition is not just global cost competitiveness, the issue for the multidimensional strategy, but also the management of global cash flow. A full product line is also needed, however. The Japanese have dominated most of the consumer electronics and appliance market by attacking RCA and Zenith in TVs. The Americans did not have the stomach for a fight in VCRs. From their U.S. profit sanctuary in VCRs, the Japanese can thus attack Whirlpool in major appliances. Whirlpool has a large share in major appliances but does not have a full line and does not have a presence in other major countries. They can fight the Japanese only in their home market. The Japanese can fund a fight from VCRs in the United States or from major appliances in Japan (or from both). Whirlpool cannot retaliate. The conclusion from the prior analysis is that global competition requires that companies be in all major international markets with a full line of products in order to manage global cash flow.

The organizational implications to managing global cash flow is that companies must be capable of acting in an integrated fashion on a global basis. In the previous example, the Japanese company must be able to reach an agreement between the VCR managers, major appliance managers, and U.S. subsidiary managers on the strategy to attack Whirlpool in the United States. This ability to work across profit centers requires coordination processes described in Chapter 5 under "Integrating Processes." In most cases, the capability will require integrating roles and matrix organization. IBM has a profit center organization in the United States with a centralized sales and service organization. The rest of the world is organized geographically around countries and regions. But some fifty worldwide product managers manage product development and worldwide profitability of their product line. Most of these managers are in the U.S. profit centers.

The organization to manage global cash flow also requires a planning process within which sources and uses of cash can be debated. It requires performance measurements and rewards to be adjusted for the subsidies. But most of all, it requires a management that thinks and acts on a global basis, not a domestic one.

The global customer is another force that is being exercised on a worldwide basis. Anyone supplying General Motors knows that it will shop the world for the lowest price. If a company has independent geographic profit centers, price differences will immediately be referred to the general manager of the business by General Motors. Hewlett-Packard has a small PC factory in Grenoble, France. It would usually receive a low priority on supply and prices from a country manager of a semiconductor supplier. But Hewlett-Packard puts pressure on the U.S. division, which in turn pressures the French country manager. Other examples could be given, but they all indicate a need to act on an integrated global basis. Independent geographic profit centers cannot be the sole basis for organizing. Since General Motors and Hewlett-Packard may buy centrally for a number of product lines, such activity must be closely coordinated. Other companies may need a global account management system throughout their sales organizations. Such companies also need performance measurement and reward systems that accommodate cross-subsidies and loss leaders across countries and across product lines. Again, matrix structures and systems appear to be the organizational policies to pursue.

The forces from global competitors, global customers, universal products, technology investments, and world-scale factories all point to more global integration. However, the countervailing forces from local governments are also strong. The global company must participate in all key countries with a full product line. These product lines and countries may not be open to companies without a negotiation with the local host government. Also, independent worldwide businesses are not effective at opening up new geography. An international division can establish relations with host governments, invest in distribution channels, brand franchises, and build an infrastructure that no single business could afford. Thus, forces still remain for local country organization. Figure 9.4 shows the trade-offs that need to be made. The various businesses and countries will locate somewhere along this continuum.

Network Organizations

Global strategies will require companies to locate somewhere near the matrix organization if all the countries and businesses are owned by the company. In a large number of instances, however,

Figure 9.4   Geography-Business Trade-Offs for Global Firms

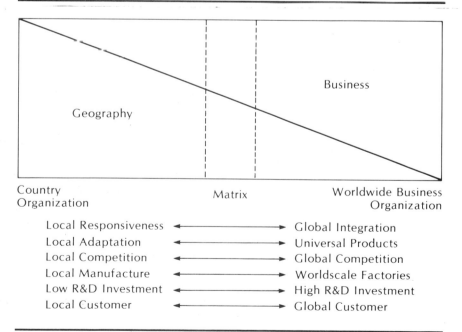

complete ownership and control will not be possible, and joint ventures, consortia, and cooperative arrangements are increasingly in evidence. On this issue, the forces of world-scale plants, large R&D investments, and active host governments are all directionally consistent.

Most companies cannot afford the technology development expense to stay at the forefront of today's rapidly advancing technology. For example, RCA and Sharp recently agreed on a joint venture that will supply each with semiconductors. RCA will contribute product technology while Sharp provides manufacturing technology. With each new advance in semiconductor technology requiring a new $100 million plant, cooperation is warranted. In like fashion, the necessary capital costs and economies of scale in the development and production of computers, semiconductors, robotics, and aircraft will require extensive use of joint ventures and other network arrangements.

Active host governments also require joint ventures of various types with local companies. To be in all key countries with a full line of products, extensive joint ventures are needed. Both economies of scale and active host governments, then, are creating the need for an extensive network of arrangements for companies. Indeed, a network organization best describes the evolving social system that must administer the global strategy.

The administration of networks of joint ventures and wholly owned subsidiaries to manage global cash flow presents enormous new problems. A network is merely a matrix organization without the ability to appeal to a tie breaker. All of the skills needed to manage a global matrix are required even more, so as to conduct business through joint ventures. Those companies who are acquiring expertise in matrix organization will be in good shape to manage through networks. Those companies who have backed away from matrix will then be at a disadvantage in global competition. Or they may become a local partner for a global company. Our view is that they will not be effective as a global company.

The global pressures are seen in those companies that are experiencing the new competition. IBM is the best example of a global American company effectively responding to the current situation. It has worldwide integrating roles that manage product lines across geographic profit centers. They are to manage product development on a global basis. Regions manage the manufacturing, although worldwide sourcing from two plants is used. Sales and service are managed by countries. They also have extensive joint ventures and equity arrangements around the world as well as research projects being conducted at universities.

MANAGING FOR INNOVATION
AND CORPORATE ENTREPRENEURSHIP

Present competitive conditions coupled with the restructuring of several major industries have forced many firms to reassess their current strategies, resulting in renewed emphasis on the topic of innovation, or what has been termed corporate entrepreneurship, directed at new products, production processes, and technologies, and the pursuit of a more diversified business mix. Such firms typically respond with a range of actions, which may include acquisitions, joint ventures, and internal development activities. Our focus here is on the latter.

Strategy and Innovation

Several types of firms must currently emphasize innovation and internal development as a prime strategic thrust. First, single- or dominant-business firms that are subject to intense competitive pressures do not have a diversified base of other businesses to perpetuate themselves. As a result, they must aggressively commit themselves to improve their competitive position if they are to survive. A similar phenomenon is experienced by such firms whose industries are maturing. Here again, competitive repositioning is critical to survival in the short run. However, both situations may lead these firms to consider diversification as well.

When considering diversification, some firms may encounter impediments to the acquisition of new businesses, and hence be driven to implement through internal development mechanisms. For example, based upon sheer size alone, some firms can expect extreme scrutiny from a range of governmental regulatory bodies when contemplating an acquisition of any size. The experience of Exxon is a case in point. As discussed in the press (Beman 1981), their bid to diversify, in part through the acquisition of Reliance Electric Company, in the late 1970s caught the attention and energies of several regulatory agencies. The impact of such restrictions slows negotiations, reduces responsiveness and can raise the price of a potential acquisition, all of which, experience demonstrates, drives such firms away from acquisition.

Second, high-technology-based firms (for example, aerospace companies conducting contract research or production tasks for the Department of Defense or NASA) working at the state of the art in various technologies, typically generate numerous new business ideas as by-products of their primary focus. In many instances, these potential new business ideas suggest either the creation of a new market or the redefinition of an existing one with radical new products or technologies. Such firms that develop a proprietary technology for a product or process are often wont to capitalize on it directly if at all, in part to protect their proprietary holdings. Harrigan (1983), for example, has discussed the reluctance of such firms to enter coalitional arrangements for fear of loss of their proprietary positions. When acquisition is considered as the entry mode in such cases, existing firms would at best offer a "shell" within which considerable focus and development would be required by the parent company to develop that new technology. Interestingly, such practices challenge the notion of acquisition versus direct entry as discrete, dichotomous choices, when in fact, they might better be thought of as a continuum.

Innovation and Organization

Our contention is that innovation requires an organization specifically designed for that purpose. Such an organization's structure, processes, rewards, and people must be combined in a special way to create an innovating organization—one that is designed to do something for the first time (Galbraith, 1982). The critical point to be noted here is that the configuration of the organizational components of the "innovating" organization are diametrically opposed to those of the organization designed for operating efficiency. As a result, firms that wish to simultaneously pursue two primary missions—efficiency of operations in existing businesses and the development of new businesses—must develop an ambidextrous capability to manage in two very different fashions within the bounds of the same organization. A comparison of organizational elements directed at operating and innovating activities is presented in Table 9.1. The contrast of each element is expanded upon next.

Structure.   The primary consideration in the selection of structure in operating settings must be viewed on two levels. First is the choice of overall form—functional, multidivisional, holding company, and so on—which is determined consistent with the firm's strategy. The logic for this choice has been thoroughly discussed in Chapters 2 and 3. Additionally, at a lower level of analysis within the primary form chosen, the firm is typically concerned with issues of how to attain efficiencies through choices of the size and task assignments to various work units or departments, the degree of specialization, and the span of control of managers. These dimensions of structure represent an appropriate bureaucratic

**Table 9.1   Comparison of Characteristics
of "Operating" and "Innovating" Organizations**

	Operating Organization	Innovating Organization
Structure	Overall Form	Primary Roles
	Division of Labor	Differentiation
	Specialization	Dedicated Functional Units
	Span of Control	IBUs
		New Venture Departments
		Development Company
Organizational Processes	Strategic Planning	Idea Generation
	Operational Budgeting	Selection and Funding
	Capital Allocation	Transitioning Ideas
	Departmental Coordination	Program Management
Rewards	Compensation	Autonomy
	Promotion	Recognition
	Job Design	Special Compensation
		Dual Ladders
People	General Managers	Idea Generators
	Specialists	Sponsors
	Professionals	Orchestrators

response to the problems of coordination and control of large, complex organizations.

For the innovating organization, however, structure must take on a very different character. First, in the early stages of the innovation process, what is called for is an absence of structure as previously discussed, as bureaucracy is anathema to innovation. Rules, regulations, procedures, accepted practice, and programmed activity will stifle creativity and drive out new ideas. As many innovative activities in large organizations center on a small number of individuals, what is needed is a small work group with the organizational climate of an independent new start-up firm, characterized by an informal, unstructured, group problem-solving approach, where decisions are made quickly and communications are personal and face-to-face. For innovations to be conceived and nurtured over time, certain critical roles are necessary (Galbraith 1982; Roberts and Fusfeld 1982). These roles then assume the function of structure for the innovating organization. Primary among these roles are three. First is the idea generator, who originally conceives of the idea that has potential as a new product, service, or process. This person is typically an individual with a breadth of experience who is close to the firm's operational problems and possible solutions. This is the creative bench-level scientist, engineering supervisor, manufacturing engineer, or marketing manager who sees a new way of doing things. Although this role is widely understood and written about, much less is known of other roles needed for the idea generator's innovation to develop.

In our view, each idea needs at least one sponsor to promote it. A sponsor is typically a middle manager who may work anywhere in the organization, but who has both operating and innovating responsibilities, and the authority and resources to carry the idea into development. Such individuals, who might be considered "bureaucratic entrepreneurs," usually know the politics of the firm, have strong selling skills, can recognize an idea with strong potential, and are personal risk takers. Their task is to support, sell, and defend the activity, providing the resources and business direction needed to move toward full adoption and implementation. The final role is that of orchestrator, who in a sense is a higher-level sponsor. This role is usually fulfilled by someone in upper management—president, executive vice-president, a division head, or the head of a functional area. This individual is not as close to the project as the sponsor, but provides legitimacy for innovative activities in general, and may intercede in support of the project itself at crucial junctures. The role is necessary to overcome the natural resistance to innovation in most large, mature firms. In such settings, innovation is both a creative and a destructive process, for the development of new activities within the firm can, in many instances, displace or obsolete existing plant, equipment, and other specialized assets, as well as alter the balance of power within the firm.

The second way in which the structure of the innovating unit differs from that of the operating organization is in its need to be differentiated from the activities of the operating units. Specifically, the development of a new idea from conception to commercialization must be buffered from the day-to-day pressures, attitudes, and biases of the existing organization, at least at the initial stages. If the focus of innovation is related to the activities of the existing organization, and if in fact the existing organization will be the implementation vehicle for the innovation, then that differentiation must lessened over time as the established ideas get transferred to the operating organization.

Such differentiated units can take a number of forms. In those cases where the new idea pertains to a new approach within the existing business of the firm, then specialized units including advanced technology groups within R&D labs, business development groups within the marketing function, or manufacturing engineering departments within production organizations may be used. However, in the case of a diversification attempt, a cross-functional project team is needed. Such teams may take the form of an independent business unit (IBU) reporting to a division or to the corporate office. The Saturn Project at General Motors as well as IBM's entrance into the personal computer market are examples of the use of IBUs. If there are enough different such activities, the firm may wish to manage them through a new ventures department. Alternatively, such departments have been created to search for new business ideas or to serve as a base for a designated group of idea generators. These groups were popular in the 1960s, but many were abandoned in the mid-1970s.

Some new ventures departments today are being structured as development companies. These subsidiaries fund ventures internal to the company and enter venture capital pools for funding outside. Also, employees can leave the company for equity arrangements with the development company. Such vehicles are usually employed only for clearly unrelated, long-term investments by the firm.

Organizational Processes. The primary processes directed at operating activities in large, complex organizations are typically directed at information sharing and decision making for both long- and short-term considerations, usually in the form of strategic planning, operational budgeting and capital allocation processes, ongoing coordination of day-to-day activities across interdependent units, and performance evaluation systems. These activities are all directed toward making the right choices about how to maximize returns of ongoing operations.

In contrast, the innovating unit has no diverse activity to plan and coordinate. Instead, processes here must be directed toward the generation, selection, funding, and development of new ideas. Examples would include Texas Instrument's well-publicized Objectives, Strategies, and Tactics (OST) system, which separates the allocation of funds for operations from those directed at innovation. Alternatively, 3M allows for the prospect of multiple funders by allowing any idea generator to request funding for the development of a new idea from any division of the company, the central R&D group, or the new ventures group. Other firms have sponsored formal events directed at matching idea generators with sponsors, or competitions to stimulate the development of new ideas.

If the focus of innovation (new product, process, and so on) will be implemented or commercialized through the operating units of the organization (as opposed to through a new organization such as an IBU), then the most critical process may well be transitioning the idea from the differentiated innovating unit to the operating unit.

This is best handled as part of the review process of the project. At each natural milestone in the development of the idea—such as proof of technological feasibility, assessment of market potential, construction of initial prototype—the firm faces a go or no-go decision requiring evaluation of progress to date and allocation of additional funds. Also, there may be a need for managerial direction regarding interaction with existing operations. At these evaluations, the firm can make choices regarding the project head, location and staffing for new tasks to be performed, where funds will come from, and how much autonomy the activity should have, which will link the project more or less closely to the operating units of the firm.

Note that these review processes may well serve two purposes. First, they are a mechanism for the evaluation of activity to date and for the determination of whether to proceed. Second, they may well serve as an education process for top management regarding the nature of the innovation currently developing, which they must subsequently manage. Many of such projects can have strategic implications for the firm and thus require top management time and attention in the review process, even though the expenditures may be relatively small early on. For example, the development of a robotics-based manufacturing process or diversification into an unrelated business could have far-reaching effects for the firm. For this reason, some firms have gone toward the design of review committees composed not just exclusively of pertinent internal management, but also including several outsiders such as consultants, academics, or managers from noncompetitive businesses (e.g., suppliers or customers) who are knowledgeable of the area in question and who can help to evaluate progress in an unbiased fashion and help top managers learn more about what they must manage in the future.

Reward Systems. The prior discussion clearly suggests that the primary tasks and desired behaviors of individuals differ in the operating versus innovating settings of the firm. Correspondingly, reward systems must reflect that difference as well. The role of rewards in operating settings has been thoroughly researched and publicized, as we reviewed in Chapter 6. However, the application of incentive and reward mechanisms to innovative settings is only now emerging as a topic of interest.

The first focus for rewards in innovating units is to the idea generator. Here, a mix of both extrinsic and intrinsic rewards is what provides incentive for the generation and development of new ideas. In part, autonomy, or the opportunity to work on one's own ideas, is a considerable reward in itself. Beyond that, however, recognition, promotion, and special compensation are also appropriate mechanisms. Recognition may come in the form of awards such as Ford's Innovator Award, the IBM Fellows Program, or the 3M Carlton Award, which are ceremoniously and publicly awarded. Such awards recognize the individual but also serve as an incentive to others while sending the clear message to the rest of the organization that innovation is a priority. Some firms have also created the practice of granting one-time cash awards, from a few dollars to tens of thousands, to individuals whose new ideas have been proven successful. In other cases, the innovator may receive a percentage of the take, such as is the case with royalties to authors of software or toy inventors. Finally, the use of a dual ladder system, which allows for promotion based upon either managerial or technical skills, is well suited to innovative settings. Such a system creates an opportunity for advancement for the idea generator who may not be managerially inclined.

Successful innovation is not dependent solely on individual idea generators. Recognizing this, a number of firms have also created group reward structures that provide a bonus to all members of the project team if the innovation activity succeeds. Other firms have formally recognized the necessity of establishing incentives for sponsors. At 3M, a portion of each division manager's bonus is based upon having 25 percent of the division's revenue coming from products introduced within the previous five years. This both rewards and provides incentive to sponsor behaviors and receptivity to new ideas.

People. A considerable body of literature exists regarding the recruitment, selection, promotion, and career development practices of firms with a primarily operational orientation, some of which has been referenced in Chapter 6. The focus of these activities, however, is directed toward the recruitment, selection, and development of functional and staff specialists, general managers, and other "professionals." A reasonable assumption, though, is that individuals well suited to operational activities are not necessarily effective at innovation, as the required tasks and associated behaviors are so different.

As previously discussed, certain roles—idea generator, sponsor, and orchestrator—are critical to the success of the innovation process. The ability of the innovating organization to generate and capitalize on new ideas can be increased by systematically developing and selecting individuals to fill these roles. Understanding the attributes and characteristics of the individuals in these roles then becomes a necessary first step.

Successful idea generators fit the pattern of stereotypical inventors. So they usually have a high need for achievement, a willingness to take risks, an irreverence for company policy and accepted practice, and a sizable ego. Such individuals typically have less of an investment in the status quo and less to lose if a change occurs. Additionally, effective idea generators have a breadth of experience both within the industry and within the firm, as well as with knowledge bases that may serve as solution and idea sources (e.g., emerging or substitute technology areas). This varied experience creates the coupling of a recognition of problems and opportunities with alternative approaches, which can result in an innovation. The retention of such individuals within the bounds of the firm will require a configuration of organizational elements as previously described.

For idea generators to succeed, however, the firm must have an adequate representation of sponsors and orchestrators. The characteristics of both are similar, although their level in the organization and closeness to the specific innovation project will differ. Such individuals typically have been described as bureacratic entrepreneurs. They have the same irreverence for the status quo but are more motivated by the prospect of the business applications and long-term implications of the idea generator's innovation. They understand the innovation process, have been exposed to it earlier in their careers, and know how to manage idea generators and task teams working on innovative projects. Additionally, they are adroit at understanding organizational politics and dynamics, and acquiring needed approvals and resources. Orchestrators, who in many instances may be former sponsors, are less tied to advocacy of specific project, as is the project's sponsor, and must take a more balanced, unbiased stance between the status quo and the innovation. However, political skills are critical here as well in the establishment of the legitimacy of the innovative activity.

SUMMARY AND MANAGERIAL IMPLICATIONS

As new problems and managerial challenges unfold, new organizational configurations must be correspondingly devised. This chapter has discussed three strategic challenges, which we believe firms will face well into the next decade, and the emerging organizational forms and administrative practices currently evolving in response. First is the management of diversity associated with increased diversification of products and markets. Here, matrix and other general management structures were discussed. The second challenge presented is the continuing globalization of markets and competition across industries. In this regard, the problems of area and worldwide product organizations were discussed, and the use of matrix and network organizations described. Finally, the necessity for innovation in the face of increasing competition and maturing industries was outlined, and the organizational characteristics of the operating and the innovating organization were contrasted.

References

Aharoni, Y. *The Foreign Investment Decision Process.* Boston: Division of Research, Harvard Business School, 1966.

Akerman, R. W. "Influence of Integration and Diversity on the Investment Process." *Administrative Science Quarterly* 15 (1970): 341–52.

Allen, S. A. "Fourth Generation Organizations: Problems, Emerging Solutions, and Human Implications." Paper presented at IEEE Systems, Man, and Cybernetics Conference, Boston, November 1973.

———. "Organizational Choices and General Management Influence Networks in Divisionalized Companies." *Academy of Management Journal* (September 1978): 341–65.

Armour, H. O., and D. J. Teece. "Organizational Structure and Economic Performance: A Test of the Multidivisional Hypothesis." *Bell Journal of Economics* 9 (Spring 1978): 106–22.

Bartlett, C. A. "MNCs: Get Off the Reorganization Merry-Go-Round." *Harvard Business Review* (March–April 1983): 138–47.

Beman, L. "Exxon's $600 Million Mistake." *Fortune,* 19 October 1981, 68–93.

Berg, N. A. "Strategic Planning in Conglomerate Companies." *Harvard Business Review* 43 (1965): 79–92.

———. "What's Different About Conglomerate Management?" *Harvard Business Review* 47 (1969): 112–20.

Bettis, R. A. "Performance Differences in Related and Unrelated Diversified Firms." *Strategic Management Journal* 2 (1981): 379–93.

171

Bettis, R. A., and W. K. Hall. "Diversification Strategy, Accounting Determined Risk, and Accounting Determined Return." *Academy of Management Journal* 25 (June 1982): 254–64.

Blau, P. M., and R. Schoenherr. *The Structure of Organizations* New York: Basic Books, 1971.

Bower, J. *The Resource Allocation Process.* Boston: Division of Research, Harvard Business School, 1970.

Burgelman, R. A. "Designs for Corporate Entrepreneurship in Established Firms." *California Management Review* 26 (Spring 1984): 154–66.

Burns, T., and G. M. Stalker. *The Management of Innovation.* London: Tavistock Publications, 1961.

Burton, R. M., and B. Obel. "A Computer Simulation Test of the M-Form Hypothesis." *Administrative Science Quarterly* 25 (September 1980): 457–66.

Cable, J., and P. Steer. "On the Industrial Organization and Profitability of Large U.K. Companies." Working paper, Liverpool Polytechnic, February 1977.

Campbell, J. P., M. D. Dunette, E. E. Lawler, and K. E. Weick. *Managerial Behavior, Performance, and Effectiveness.* New York: McGraw-Hill, 1970.

Chandler, A. D. *Strategy and Structure.* Cambridge, Mass.: MIT Press, 1962.

Channon, D. *The Strategy and Structure of British Enterprise.* London: MacMillan and Co., 1973.

———. "Strategy, Structure, and Performance in the British Service Industries." Unpublished manuscript, 1977.

Child, J. "Organization Structure, Environment, and Performance: The Role of Strategic Choice." *Sociology* 6 (1972): 1–22.

———. "Managerial and Organizational Factors Associated with Company Performance—Part I." *Journal of Management Studies* (October 1974): 175–89.

———. "Managerial and Organizational Factors Associated with Company Performance—Part II, A Contingency Analysis." *Journal of Management Studies* (February 1975): 12–27.

———. *Organization: A Guide for Managers and Administrators.* New York: Harper & Row, 1977.

Child, J., and A. Keiser. "The Development of Organizations Over Time." In *Handbook of Organization Design,* vol. 1, edited by P. Nystrom and W. Starbuck. Amsterdam: Elsevier/North Holland, 1978.

Child J., and R. Mansfield. "Technology, Size, and Organization Structure." *Sociology* 6 (1972): 369–93.

Christensen, H. K., and C. A. Montgomery. "Corporate Economic Performance: Diversification Strategy Versus Market Structure." *Strategic Management Journal* 2 (1981): 327–43.

Corey, E. R., and S. H. Star. *Organization Strategy*. Boston: Division of Research, Harvard Business School, 1971.

Cyert, R., and J. March. *The Behavioral Theory of the Firm*. Englewood Cliffs, N.J.: Prentice-Hall, 1963.

Davidson, W. H., and P. Haspeslagh. "Shaping a Global Product Organization." *Harvard Business Review* (July–August 1982): 125–32.

Dundas, K. N. M., and P. R. Richardson. "Corporate Strategy and The Concept of Market Failure." *Strategic Management Journal* 1 (1980): 177–88.

———. "Implementing the Unrelated Product Strategy." *Strategic Management Journal* 3 (1982): 287–301.

Edstrom, A., and J. Galbraith. "Transfer of Managers as a Coordination and Control Strategy in Multi-National Organizations." *Administrative Science Quarterly* 22 (1977): 248–63.

Fouraker, L. E., and J. M. Stopford. "Organization Structure and Multinational Strategy." *Administrative Science Quarterly* (June 1968): 57–70.

Franko, L. "The Move Toward a Multi-Divisional Structure in European Organizations." *Administrative Science Quarterly* 19 (1974): 493–506.

———. *The European Multinationals*. Greenwich, Conn.: Greylock Press, 1976.

Fry, L. W. "Technology-Structure Research: Three Critical Issues." *Academy of Management Journal* (1982): 532–52.

Galbraith, J. R. *Designing Complex Organizations*. Reading, Mass.: Addison-Wesley, 1973.

———. *Organization Design*. Reading, Mass.: Addison-Wesley, 1977.

———. "Strategy and Organization Planning." *Human Resource Management* 22 (Spring/Summer 1983): 63–77.

———. "Designing the Innovating Organization." *Organizational Dynamics* 10 (1982): 5–25.

Galbraith, J. R., and D. A. Nathanson. *Strategy Implementation: The Role of Structure and Process*. St. Paul: West, 1978.

Gerwin, D. "Relationships between Structure and Technology at the Organizational and Job Levels." *Journal of Management Studies* (February 1979): 70–79.

Goggins, W. "How the Multi-Dimensional Structure Works at Dow-Corning." *Harvard Business Review* 52 (1974): 54–65.

Grinyer, P. H., and M. Yasai-Ardekani. "Dimensions of Organizational Structure: A Critical Replication." *Academy of Management Journal* 23 (1980): 405–21.

———. "Strategy, Structure, Size, and Bureaucracy." *Academy of Management Journal* 24 (3) (1981): 471–86.

Gupta, A. "Contingency Linkages Between Strategy and General Manager Characteristics." *Academy of Management Review* 9 (1984): 399–412.

Gupta, A., and V. Govindarajan. "Business Unit Strategy, Managerial Characteristics, and Business Unit Effectiveness at Strategy Implementation." *Academy of Management Journal* 27 (March 1984): 25–41.

Hall, D. T. *Careers in Organizations.* Santa Monica, Calif.: Goodyear, 1976.

Hamel, G., and C. K. Prahalad. "Do You Really Have A Global Strategy?" *Harvard Business Review* 63 (4) (1985): 139–48.

Hannan, M., and J. Freeman. "Structural Inertia and Organizational Change." *American Sociological Review* 49 (April 1984): 149–64.

Harrigan, K. R. "Strategies for Joint Ventures." Working paper, Strategy Center, Columbia University, 1983.

Haspeslagh, P. "Portfolio Planning: Uses and Limits." *Harvard Business Review* (January–February 1982): 58–73.

Hinings, C. R., and G. L. Lee. "Dimensions of Organization Structure and their Context: A Replication." *Sociology* 5 (1971): 83–93.

Hitt, M. A., R. D. Ireland, and K. A. Palia. "Industrial Firms, Grand Strategy, and Functional Importance: Moderating Effects of Technology and Uncertainty." *Academy of Management Journal* 25 (1982): 265–98.

Hofer, C. W. *Strategy Formulation: Issues and Concepts.* 2d ed. St. Paul: West, 1986.

Kazanjian, R. K. "The Organizational Evolution of High Technology Ventures: The Impact of Stage of Growth on the Nature of Structure and Planning Processes." Ph.D. diss., The Wharton School, University of Pennsylvania, 1983.

Kerr, J. "Assigning Managers on the Basis of the Life Cycle." *Journal of Business Strategy* 2 (Spring 1982): 58–65.

———. "Diversification Strategies and Managerial Rewards: An Empirical Study." *Academy of Management Journal* 28 (March 1985): 155–79.

Kilmann, R., and I. Mitroff. "On Organization Stories: An Approach to the Design and Analysis of Organizations Through Myths and Stories." In *The Management of Organization Design*, vol. 1, edited by R. Kilmann, L. R. Pondy, and D. P. Slevin. Amsterdam: Elsevier/North Holland, 1976.

Kotler, P., L. Fahey, and S. Jatusripitak. *The New Competition*. Engelwood Cliffs, N.J.: Prentice-Hall, 1985.

Kotter, J. P. *The General Managers*. New York: Free Press, 1982.

Lawler, E. "Adaptive Experiments—An Approach to Organizational Behavior Research." *Academy of Management Review* 2 (1977): 576–85.

———. "Reward Systems." In *Improving Life at Work*, edited by Hackman and Suttle. Santa Monica, Calif.: Goodyear, 1977.

Lawrence, P., and S. Davis. *Matrix*. Reading, Mass.: Addison-Wesley, 1978.

Lawrence, P., and J. Lorsch. *Organization and Environment*. Boston: Division of Research, Harvard Business School, 1967.

———. *Developing Organizations: Diagnosis and Action*. Reading, Mass.: Addison-Wesley, 1969.

Leavitt, H. "Unhuman Organizations." *Harvard Business Review*, (July–August 1962): 90–98.

———. "Applied Organizational Change in Industry." In *The Handbook of Organizations*, edited by James March. Chicago: Rand McNally, 1965.

Lenz, R. T. " 'Determinants' of Organizational Performance: An Interdisciplinary Review." *Strategic Management Journal* 2 (1981): 131–54.

Leontiades, M. *Strategies for Diversification and Change*. Boston: Little, Brown, 1980.

Lippman, S. A., and R. P. Rumelt. "Uncertain Imitability: An Analysis of Interfirm Differences in Efficiency Under Competition." *Bell Journal of Economics* 13 (1982): 418–38.

Lorange, P. *Corporate Planning: An Executive Viewpoint*. Englewood Cliffs, N. J.: Prentice-Hall, 1980.

Lorange, P., M. Scott Morton, and S. Ghoshal. *Strategic Control Systems.* St. Paul: West, 1986.

Lorsch, J., and S. Allen. *Managing Diversity and Interdependence.* Boston: Division of Research, Harvard Business School, 1973.

Lorsch, J., and J. Morse. *Organizations and Their Members.* New York: Harper & Row, 1974.

Maidique, M. A., and P. Patch. "Corporate Strategy and Technological Policy." In *Readings in the Management of Innovation,* edited by M. L. Tushman and W. L. Moore, Boston: Pitman, 1982, 273–85.

Mauriel, J., and R. Anthony. "Misevaluation of Investment Center Performance." *Harvard Business Review* 44 (1966): 98–105.

McCaskey, M. "Tolerance for Ambiguity and the Perception of Environmental Uncertainty in Organization Design." In *The Management of Organization Design,* vol. 2, edited by R. Kilmann, L. R. Pondy, and D. P. Slevin. Amsterdam: Elsevier/North Holland, 1976.

McKelvey, B., and H. Aldrich. "Populations, Natural Selection, and Applied Organizational Science." *Administrative Science Quarterly* (March 1983): 101–28.

Meyer, H. "The Pay-for-Performance Dilemma." *Organization Dynamics* (Winter 1975): 39–50.

Miles, R., and C. Snow. *Environmental Strategy and Organization Structure.* New York: McGraw-Hill, 1978.

———. "Fit, Failure, and the Hall of Fame." *California Management Review* 26 (Spring 1984): 10–28.

Miles, R. H., and K. S. Cameron. "Coffin Nails and Corporate Strategies: A Quarter Century View of Organizational Adaptation to Environment in the U.S. Tobacco Industry." Working Paper no. 3, Business-Government Relations Series (c). New Haven, Conn.: Yale School of Organization and Management, 1977.

Miles, R. H. *Coffin Nails and Corporate Strategies.* Englewood Cliffs, N.J.: Prentice-Hall, 1982.

Miller, D. "Toward a New Contingency Approach: The Search for Organizational Gestalts." *Journal of Management Studies* 18 (1981): 1–26.

Miller, D., and P. Friesen. "Archetypes of Organizational Transition." *Administrative Science Quarterly* 25 (1980a): 268–99.

———. "Momentum and Revolution in Organizational Adaptation." *Academy of Management Journal* 23 (1980b): 591–614.

Mohr, L. B. "Organization Technology and Organization Structure." *Administrative Science Quarterly* 16 (1971): 444–59.

Morse, J., and D. Young. "Personality Development and Task Choices: A Systems View." *Human Relations* 26 (1973): 307–24.

Nathanson, D. A. "The Relationship Between Situational Factors, Organizational Characteristics, and Firm Performance." Ph. D. diss., The Wharton School, University of Pennsylvania, 1980.

Nathanson, D. A., and J. Cassano. "What Happens to Profits When a Company Diversifies?" *Wharton Magazine* (Summer 1982): 19–26.

Norburn, D., and P. Miller. "Strategy and Executive Reward: The Mis-Match in the Strategic Process." *Journal of General Management* 6 (Summer 1981): 17–27.

Pennings, J. "The Relevance of the Structural-Contingency Model for Organizational Effectiveness." *Administrative Science Quarterly* 20 (1975): 393–410.

Penrose, E. T. *The Theory of the Growth of the Firm.* New York: Wiley, 1959.

Peters, T. J., and R. H. Waterman, Jr. *In Search of Excellence.* New York: Harper & Row, 1982.

Pitts, R. A. "Strategies and Structures for Diversification." *Academy of Management Journal* 20 (1977): 197–208.

Pitts, R. A., and D. H. Hopkins. "Firm Diversity: Conceptualization and Measurement." *Academy of Management Review* 7 (October 1982): 620–29.

Poensgen, O. "Organizational Structure, Context, and Performance." Working paper no. 74–49, European Institute for Advanced Studies in Management, November 1974.

Pooley-Dyas, G. "Strategy and Structure of French Enterprise." Ph.D. diss., Harvard Business School, 1972.

Porter, M. *Competitive Strategy.* New York: Free Press, 1980.

Prahalad, C. K., and Y. L. Doz. "An Approach to Strategic Control in MNCs." *Sloan Management Review,* (Summer 1981): 5–13.

Pugh, D. S., D. J. Hickson, and C. R. Hinings. "An Empirical Taxonomy of Structures of Work Organizations." *Administrative Science Quarterly* 14 (1969): 115–126.

Pugh, D. S., D. J. Hickson, C. R. Hinings, K. M. Macdonald, C. Turner, and T. Lupton. "A Conceptual Scheme for Organizational Analysis." *Administrative Science Quarterly* 8 (December 1963): 289–315.

————. "Dimensions of Organization Structure." *Administrative Science Quarterly* 13 (June 1968): 65–105.

Rappaport, A. "Executive Incentives vs. Corporate Growth." *Harvard Business Review* (July–August 1978): 81–88.

————. "Selecting Strategies That Create Shareholder Value." *Harvard Business Review* (May–June 1981): 139–49.

————. "Corporate Performance Standards and Shareholder Value." *Journal of Business Strategy* 3 (Spring 1983): 28–38.

————. "How to Design Value—Contributing Executive Incentives." *Journal of Business Strategy* 4 (Fall 1983): 49–59.

Richards, M. D. *Organizational Goal Structures.* St. Paul: West, 1978.

————. *Setting Strategic Goals and Objectives.* 2d ed. St. Paul: West, 1986.

Roberts, E. B., and A. R. Fusfeld. "Critical Functions: Needed Roles in the Innovation Process." In *Career Issues in Human Resource Management,* edited by R. Katz. Englewood Cliffs, N. J.: Prentice-Hall, 1982.

Rumelt, R. P. *Strategy, Structure, and Economic Performance.* Boston: Division of Research, Harvard Business School, 1974.

————. "Diversity and Profitability." Paper presented at the Academy of Management Western Region meetings, Sun Valley, Idaho, April 1977.

————. "Diversification Strategy and Profitability." *Strategic Management Journal* 3 (1982): 359–69.

Rumelt, R. P., and R. Wensley. "In Search of the Market Share Effect." *Academy of Management Proceedings* (1981): 2–6.

Salter, M. "Stages of Corporate Development." *Journal of Business Policy* 1 (1970): 40–57.

————. "Tailor Incentive Compensation to Strategy." *Harvard Business Review* 51 (1973): 94–102.

Scott, B. R. "Stages of Corporate Development." 9-371-294, BP 998, Intercollegiate Case Clearinghouse, Harvard Business School, 1971.

————. "The Industrial State: Old Myths and New Realities." *Harvard Business Review* 51 (1973): 133–48.

Smith, G. "Culture Shift." *Forbes,* 26 October 1983, 68–71.

Smith, W., and R. Charmoz. "Coordinate Line Management." Working paper, Searle International, Chicago, February 1975.

Snow, C. C., and L. G. Hrebiniak. "Strategy, Distinctive Competence, and Organizational Performance." *Administrative Science Quarterly* 25 (1980): 317–35.

Song, J. H. "Diversification Strategies and the Experience of Top Executives of Large Firms." *Strategic Management Journal* 25 (1982): 377–80.

Starbuck, W. "Organizational Growth and Development." In *Handbook of Organization*, edited by J. G. March. Chicago: Rand McNally, 1965.

———. *Organizational Growth and Development*. London: Penguin, 1971.

Stonich, P. J. "Using Rewards in Implementing Strategy." *Strategic Management Journal* 2 (1981): 345–52.

Stonich, P. J., and C. E. Zaragoza. "Strategic Funds Programming: The Missing Link in Corporate Planning." *Managerial Planning* (September–October 1980): 3–11.

Stopford, J. "Growth and Organizational Change in the Multi-National Field." Ph.D. diss., Harvard Business School, 1968.

Stopford, J., and L. Wells. *Managing the Multinational Enterprise*. London: Longmans, 1972.

Suzuki, Y. "The Strategy and Structure of Top 100 Japanese Industrial Enterprises 1950–1970." *Strategic Management Journal* 1 (1980): 265–91.

Teece, D. J. "Internal Organization and Economic Performance: An Empirical Analysis of the Profitability of Principal Firms." *Journal of Industrial Economics* (December 1981): 173–99.

———. "Economies of Scope and the Scope of the Enterprise." *Journal of Economic Behavior and Organization* 1 (1980): 223–47.

Thompson, J. D. *Organizations in Action*. New York: McGraw-Hill, 1967.

Tichy, N. M., C. J. Fombrun, and M. A. Devanna. "Strategic Human Resource Management." *Sloan Management Review* (Winter 1982): 47–61.

Tregoe, B., and J. Zimmerman. *Top Management Strategy*. New York: Simon & Schuster, 1980.

Van Maanen, J., and E. Schein. "Career Development." In *Improving Life at Work*, edited by Hackman and Suttle. Santa Monica, Calif.: Goodyear, 1977.

Waterman, R. H., T. J. Peters, and J. R. Phillips. "Structure is Not Organization." *McKinsey Quarterly* (Summer 1980): 2–21.

Watson, C. "Counter-Competition Abroad to Protect Home Markets." *Harvard Business Review* (January–February 1982): 40–45.

Weber, M. *The Theory of Social and Economic Organization.* Glencoe, Ill.: Free Press, 1947.

Wernerfelt, B. "A Resource-Based View of the Firm." *Strategic Management Journal* 5 (April–June 1984): 171–80.

Williamson, O. *Corporate Control and Business Behavior.* Englewood Cliffs, N.J.: Prentice-Hall, 1970.

———. *Markets and Hierarchies.* New York: Free Press, 1975.

———. "Transaction-Cost Economics: The Governance of Contractual Relations." *Journal of Law and Economics* (October 1979): 233–61.

Woodward, J. *Industrial Organization: Theory and Practice.* London: Oxford University Press, 1965.

Wrigley, L. "Divisional Autonomy and Diversification." Ph.D. diss., Harvard Business School, 1970.

INDEX